Almost Something

Francy Deniehy

Copyright © 2025 by Francy Deniehy

All rights reserved.

No portion of this book may be reproduced in any form without written permission from the publisher or author, except as permitted by U.S. copyright law.

Contents

1. Prologue — 1
2. Chapter 1 — 5
3. Chapter 2 — 10
4. Chapter 3 — 15
5. Chapter 4 — 19
6. Chapter 5 — 24
7. Chapter 6 — 32
8. Chapter 7 — 37
9. Chapter 8 — 42
10. Chapter 9 — 49
11. Chapter 10 — 55
12. Chapter 11 — 61
13. Chapter 12 — 71
14. Chapter 13 — 77
15. Chapter 14 — 87
16. Chapter 15 — 94
17. Chapter 16 — 106
18. Chapter 17 — 112

19.	Chapter 18	123
20.	Chapter 19	132
21.	Chapter 20	141
22.	Chapter 21	149
23.	Chapter 22	154
24.	Chapter 23	161
25.	Chapter 24	168
26.	Chapter 25	175
27.	Chapter 26	181
28.	Chapter 27	186
29.	Epilogue	191

1

Prologue

Alison and Ryan have been friends for years now. They are the best of friends. There isn't anything they don't know about each other except maybe that they have feelings for each other. Alison has never had a boyfriend, and Ryan on the other hand has had many girlfriends before. They were different from each other. Ryan didn't really believe that there was one person that was out there for him but Alison knew that somewhere out there, there was a guy that she would spend the rest of her life with. She knew that he was out there. One day Alison meets a guy named Christopher. He's nice, handsome, tall, and very smart. He treats her like a princess. She knew that he was the one for her so she decided to introduce him to her friends.

So on the night they decide to have dinner she invites Christopher over as a surprise. "Hey guys, this is Christopher. My.... Boyfriend." Although she struggles to say the B word she's still very happy to declare him hers. And Christopher was happy too, he smiled at her sincerely as he rubbed her lower back. Ryan could see the way she looked at him. "She really likes him" Ryan thought as he looked down disappointed but he didn't know why he was disappointed. The rest of her friends were just in shock but also happy for her.

They had those cheesy smiles that girls have when they see a cute lovey dovey scene in a movie. They couldn't speak. "Ahem!..... guys! Are you here?" In unison, "Yeah! .. we're just... just.... Surprised that's all." They still had that cheesy smile. Alison saw Ryan looking down. "Ryan? Are you okay?"

Ryan's POV

My head immediately shot up as soon as I heard her voice. I just stared at her and then I stared at Christopher's arm around her waist. I was feeling... jealous? I didn't know why it bothered me so much. I mean.... Why should I be jealous? She's my friend.

It's not like she's my girlfriend. I guess I just keep thinking of her as my Alison. I knew she wouldn't be single forever cause I mean look at her, she's gorgeous. She's the most beautiful girl I've ever seen and she doesn't even wear makeup. She's so amazing and she doesn't even try. She's just that girl. I always knew guys would be trying to date her but I just thought that she was too good for any guy. I didn't think I'd see the day that she'd bring a guy over and introduce him as her boyfriend. I guess you can say I was really surprised. I didn't realize I was still staring until she started waving her hand in front of my face. "Oh... uh." I stuttered. She tilted her head, "Ryan, are you okay" she said as she looked at me with concern. I hated it when she did that, it made me concerned. "Ye-yeah. I'm fine." After a few minutes the shock began to subside and we just accepted it. Alison was no longer single. She found her... guy? I don't know what else to say. She found that guy she knew was out there. Of course I don't think there is that one person out there but if I did I didn't think it would be him. I don't know what it was, but I couldn't picture him with her forever. The thought just sickened me.

But I sucked it up, I couldn't be jealous of this forever. Could I?When Christopher left, Alison came outside to talk to me. She hopped onto the balcony with a beaming smile. She was so cute when she was happy and every other time. I couldn't help but smile back. She sat next to me and nudged me in the arm."So....????!!!??""So... what?"She rolled her eyes, "Oh come on! What'd you think about Christopher????""He's nice." I told her. And I was being completely honest. He was nice. That's it, nothing special.Her jaw dropped and she looked at me like I was crazy, "Nice???? That's all!""Yeah.... What else am I suppose to say?""That he's perfect for me? That he's amazing?""Alison... no one is perfect or amazing enough to be with you."She frowns. And I can't help but laugh."Stop laughing. It's not funny! I brought him over cause I knew he was a great guy for me." "I'm sorry, but again... no guy is great enough to be with you. He doesn't deserve you, no guy does.""Oh come on, he's amazing.""I don't know what all the fuss is about? He's just a regular guy. Nothing special.""Nothing special???? He's not only tall, handsome and smart, but he's so so kind and loving."Hearing her talk about him like that saddened me. I didn't like that she was falling for a guy that was mediocre. She deserves better.

Alison's POV

I don't know why Ryan thought Christopher was just a regular guy. I mean, how could he? Christopher's amazing. He kept saying that he was just mediocre and regular.... That does not describe Christopher. It's almost like he was jealous. It was weird.Then he said, "Fine, he's alright I guess.""You'll see. Next time I bring him over you'll get to know him."He gave me an unconvinced look, "We'll see.""Haha okay. How about you huh???" I poked hi gently, "Where's your weekly muse?""Weekly muse?""Yeah... you always have a new girl every week. It's kind of your routine." "No I don't." He defended "Actually... you do." "I don't know what you're talking about." "Oh come on, we've been friends for years now, I think I know you pretty well by now. So where is she huh? Meeting at our house for a late night booty call?" "I don't have a girl right now." "Pleasssseee. You always have a girl!" "Not tonight." "Don't lie to me. Your girls are always the skanky kind. The one's that touch you everywhere when you're in public."

Ryan's POV

Alison starts to touch me on my chest and on my thigh. She always did this when she was making fun of the girls I "date" and it never bothered me. But this time I started to get nervous and I don't know why. Every time she brushed her fingers against me I just wanted to get closer to her. I wanted to... touch her too, but I couldn't she was Christopher's not my Alison anymore. I couldn't take the way she was touching me anymore, if it went on any longer I would lose control so I grabbed her wrists. She looked at me with a cute smile on her face. She knew it turned me on. "Ooooo, you were turned on, weren't you?" she says wiggling her eyebrows "No, I just... I just think you shouldn't be touching me like that when you have a boyfriend." "Oh yeah right. I saw how uncomfortable I made you feel. You liked it." "No, I didn't. Come on you're Alison." "Yeah, I know that. And you love me." The way she said, "You love me" didn't sound crazy at all. It actually had some truth to it. I know I love her as a friend but not more than that. I mean I couldn't love her as more than a friend... could I?

2

Chapter 1

Ryan's POV

As I'm waiting at the house for Alison for our weekly dinner, I start to look through some pictures of us. If someone else came into the house and looked at the photos they would've guessed Alison and I were dating, but they'd be wrong. Sure, it looked like we were but the truth is, she had someone else and someone else had her. I had no one and no one had me. I stare at this photo of us at the beach. It was suppose to be just a photo of her, but I remember I grabbed her from behind and hugged her. She looked at me and I looked at her and snap! It was a picture of us hugging, looking at each other with smiles. I don't remember most things, but as I look through the pictures I remember almost everything. I remember every time I was with her. It was strange, I never realized it until now. Then suddenly the door slams and I look up. It's Alison, she looks like she's in a hurry. She gives me an excited smile and takes off her jacket and shoes she runs up the stairs and into her room. I run after her and say, "So what are we doing tonight?"

"Well... I'm going out."

"Out? Where?"

"I'm gonna have dinner with Christopher in like an hour so I have to hurry."

"What? You aren't going to spend tonight with me?"

"Aw, Ryan, I can't. I already said yes. You understand right?"

"Ahh it's okay have fun."

"Thank you. I'll make it up to you. I promise!" With that she ran up to me and kissed me on the cheek and hurried into the shower. I went to my room and just listened to some music. Jasmine, this girl I've been hanging out with for the past couple of weeks was texting me but I didn't want to answer. She would want to hangout but I wasn't up for it. Then without warning she was at my door. She ran over to me and gave me a kiss on the cheek.

"Jasmine! What are you doing here?"

"I texted you."

"I didn't check my phone."

"Well it's right next to you."

"I didn't see it."

"Well, I'm here now. Let's do something."

As she said that she straddled me and started to kiss me. I sigh and pull away and say, "I just wanna stay home tonight."

"Fine, then I'll stay with you, I know exactly what we could do." she winked at me and started to kiss my neck. As nice as Jasmine is, sometimes she's just too easy. I start to look through my phone trying to ignore her but she keeps putting her hands through my hair and looking at me so intently. I hear heels tap against the hard wood floor. I know it's not Jasmine cause she's on top of me. And I know Anna isn't home it must be Alison. I look towards that hallway and see Alison walk past. She was wearing a short black dress but not one that looked indecent. It wasn't too tight, it hugged her body in all the right places. She never wore heels or dresses like that. I was really ... what's the word... in awe? Turned on? She went back and forth between her and Anna's room borrowing stuff. Then she saw me and Jasmine in my room. She wasn't surprised because she's seen me with lots of girls like this. She just sweetly smiled and said, "Hey Jasmine, how are you?"

"Good and how are you? You look hot! Where are you going?"

"I'm going out with my boyfriend tonight."

"You have a boyfriend now?"

"Yeah, his name is Christopher."

"Aww, that's great!"

"So how do I look?" she twirls around and does a little curtsey like what princesses do. I just loss my breath. I was speechless.

Alison's POVJasmine immediately says, "You look amazing! I never knew you had such a sexy body. Look at that tiny waist! You should dress like this more often. Don't you think Ryan?"

I laugh and smile. I wait for Ryan to speak but it looks like he's just staring. It kind of made me uncomfortable. He's never looked at me like this before, it's weird. It was almost as if he was checking me out."Ryan? What do you think?" I said

"You-you look so beautiful."When he said that he almost looked heartbroken, like someone stabbed him in the back.I was running late, and I still had to put on some makeup. So I ran over to my room and said back, "Thanks. I'll see you two later. BEHAVE!"Ryan and his girls, not one girl would say no to him. He's just too good. He's so good looking it would be crazy to not lust after him. Trust me, I know I've known him for years now and now I'm just immune to his sexiness.The doorbell rings, oh crap, I'm not ready yet. I rush over to the door and open it somewhat out of breath. I swing the door open and there he is, his mouth was open. I smiled and touched my finger to his chin to close it. He just smiled and looked at me with meaningful eyes. "Alison, you look gorgeous."

"You're just realizing that now?"

He chuckled, "Silly me." He pulled me into a tight hug and buried his face into my hair.

When we get to the restaurant he puts his arm around my waist and guides me to our table. He pulls out the chair for me and pushes it in as I sit down.

"We've been together for 3 months now and I'm so glad I have you."

"Me too. Everything has been great"

"Really? Cause I feel like I'm enjoying this more than you are."

"What are you talking about?"

"I mean, I know I feel a spark between us, but I don't know if you do."

"I know I like you, a lot. There doesn't always have to be a spark."

"I like you a lot too, but there should be at least a little spark between us right?"

"I don't know what to say."

"I'm falling for you, Alison. And I know that there is a great possibility that I love you now. I can even see a future with us. But I don't know if you can do the same."

"It's too soon to tell."

"I'm not saying that I want to break up, but I just want to know if you can actually picture us being together in the future. That's all I need to know."

"I don't know yet."

"I'm willing to wait, but please... if you don't, tell me."

"I promise." With that he kisses me and I feel... nothing. Nada. I don't feel that spark he was talking about.

3

CHAPTER 2

Ryan's POV

As I'm laying in bed with Jasmine next me, I think of how little sex with her meant to me. I know she likes me but I don't like her that way. She just throws herself at me and all I do is use her. She's nothing to me and I feel bad, but what else am I going to do? I don't have any other girl I want to be with. I go to the kitchen in just my boxers to get some water. I start to think about how I've been with girl after girl and still felt nothing. What's it going to take for me to care? I haven't even found one girl I care about. Then I hear the door unlock slowly and quietly, it's Alison trying to be sneaky. It's 3am in the morning, what the hell Alison? What are you doing out so late?

"Wow... you are so not 007." At first she jumps and once she sees its me she smiles.

"Haha, shut up. I tried."

She relaxes and takes off her shoes and walks over to me. You'd think that at 3am she'd look tired and that her makeup would run off her face but she still looked great. She grabbed the glass of water out of my hands and drank it. All I did was smile, we always felt comfortable around each other. Well at least until she introduced her boyfriend.

"So... looks like you had fun tonight. You're just in your boxers." she says pointing at my boxers.

"Fun? Nah... it was okay."

"Just okay?" she raises an eyebrow.

"Yeah, like every other time."

"Why is it that when you sleep with a girl, it's just "okay"?"

"I don't know. It just is."

"Haha mhmm."

"What mhmm?"

"Just mhmm." She playful shook her head as she said that to me. She was so cute.

"What about you, huh? Look at the back of your head. Looks like sex hair."

"What? What are you talking about?" She pats the back of her head and looks embarrassed.

"Hey, it's okay. Everyone has sex."

"Not me. We're not even that serious."

"What?"

"We haven't done it" she whispers.

"Wow... really?"

"Mhmm".

Then it was silent for a while.

"Why haven't you guys done it?" I spit out

"I just, I just think that it should be with someone I love."

She didn't love him? I feel so relieved. I actually have a chance. Wait what? What am I thinking? I can't be thinking about wanting to be with her. It's Alison, stupid. She's your friend.

Alison's POV

He was quiet for a moment. As long as Ryan and I have been friends, we've never talked about sex. He looked at me intently, his eyes were piercing through me. I had to look away. Then he just coughed to break the ice and said, "So I think I should go back to bed."

"Yeah, I should go to bed too."

As I walk up the stairs I feel so confused. Ryan and I have been having these awkward moments lately and it was bothering me. We've always been so comfortable when it comes to everything but all of a sudden when we talk about relationships and sex things get weird. I must've spent 2 hours in the shower just thinking about Ryan and how awkward everything was. I think back to when things first got awkward and it was when I first brought Christopher over. He's being acting weird since then and it has caused me to act weirdtoo. And when I went to bed I still couldn't stop thinking about it. It kept me up the whole night. I didn't get sleep that night. It was 8am already and I haven't even slept one minute. I decide to get up thinking that no one is up yet. I go downstairs and find Ryan watching tv. He sees me walking down the stairs. Oh no, awkward again. I can't just go back to my room he already saw me. I walk over to the kitchen to make some coffee. I can feel his eyes burning the head of my head.

"Stop looking at me." I say somewhat bitterly.

"What? How'd you know I was looking at you."

"We've been friends for a long time Ryan. I know."

"Oh..." he says shyly

"So why were you burning a whole in my head with your eyes."

"I wasn't-"

"Yes you were." I cut him off

"Okay... I just, I mean. The air around us was just weird. I didn't know what to say."

I didn't expect him to say that. I thought he would try to deny it again.

"I know! It's weird now and I have no idea why. I don't like it."

"I don't like it either. What should we do?" Aww, he looks like a sad puppy.

"Let's just move past it. I miss us just talking about random stuff and laughing. We were always comfortable with each other, let's just forget whatever's been bothering us. I mean, come on... it's us."

"Yeah, I miss it too. It is us... we're Ryan and Alison. Let's just get back to it."

"Thank goodness. I couldn't sleep thinking about how weird it was."

"Me too. So I just went here to try to forget."

"You always watch tv when you can't sleep."

"And you always get something from the kitchen to get something to take your mind off whatever is keeping you up."

"Haha I know. Here I'll make you some coffee."

"Thanks."

Ryan's POV

She walked over to the living room and set the mugs down on the coffee table. I tapped the seat next to me and opened my arm. She smiled and snuggled up to me. She put her head on my shoulder and said, "I'm so glad you're my best friend, Ryan." She looked up at me and smiled. I couldn't speak. Lately her smiles have seem to jumble up my thoughts and make me weak in the knees. I managed to give her a smile back and she continued to watch the television.

How am I suppose to just be her friend when every little thing she does makes my heart skip a beat?

4

CHAPTER 3

Ryan's POV

Lately things have been okay with me and Alison. For the past couple of weeks, we haven't seen much of each other. Sometimes, she sleeps over at Christopher's place and sometimes he sleeps over at our house. When he sleeps over, I call up Jasmine and sleep over at her place. I know I'd go crazy if I stayed when he slept over. My mind would just keep thinking about what they were doing behind closed doors. My mind already wonders about that stuff when I'm in Jasmine's bed. I don't like knowing that he's the one that gets to make love to her. I wish it was me and it breaks my heart. Why didn't I realize my feelings for her before? We've tried to push aside what was bothering us but there is still some weirdness in the air. I can feel it. I feel like she's holding back and trying to keep her distance when it comes to being with me and I've been doing the same. I guess I'm just scared things will happen that might break our friendship, I can never let that happen. I can't lose her. Sometimes Christopher comes over and it doesn't bother me, but sometimes I see them cuddling and that's when I get really irritated. I mean how hard is it to not do that stuff in front of me? Okay, I haven't told her how I felt but sometimes the girl is so clueless. She should already know that I want to be with her, but she doesn't see it. It's not their fault. There they are. Christopher is laying there on OUR couch and Alison is on top of him. He has his arm draped over her waist. They're just watching tv, why do they have to do that? As I'm caught up in my own thoughts and Christopher gets up and says, "I gotta go."

'Finally' I think to myself. He's been here for the whole freaking day, doesn't he have a life?

"Okay, I'll walk you out." Alison says.

"Hey Ryan, I'll see you man."

"Yeahhh... bye." I say, sounding a little too happy.

I don't see them outside but I can bet that she's kissing him goodbye. F M L

Alison's POV

As I walk Christopher out I spit out, "Chris, I can't do this."

He walks over to me and says, "What do you mean?"

"I don't feel that spark you were talking about."

"Oh." he looks down.

"I want to. I really do, I've waited to see if it would happen, but it hasn't."

"I understand."

"I'm sorry. I really want to fall for you, but I'm just not."

"Alison... it's okay. Really, I'm fine. I'm just glad that you gave it a chance. Thank you."

"But Chris..."

"It's okay... don't worry. I'm just so glad I got to know you. You're an amazing girl. And I'm glad we're friends."

"We're just friends, aren't we?"

"We are. And I'm fine with that."

"Thank you so much Chris."

"No thank you. I'll keep in touch, friend." He gives me an endearing smile and kisses my hand. He's such a gentleman and I'm so sad that he wasn't that guy I thought he was. I wish he was that guy but he isn't. I start crying and he immediately comes to my side to wipe away my tears. I smile weakly and push his hands away. "What is it?" he asks

"I just ... I just don't want to lose you as a friend."

He smiles at me and gently brushes my cheek and says, "You'll never lose me." Then he pulls me in for a warm long hug. I rest my head on his shoulder. He let's go and tilts his head to look at me and says, "Don't cry. You broke up with me, remember? I'm the one that should be crying." he smiles. I let out a weak laugh at his attempt to make me smile. He kisses my forehead and says, "I'll be here for you, okay? And if ever you decide you want to give us a try again, I'll be there." I sigh and smile a little. He gets in his car and starts the engine. Why can't I love him? He's everything I want and more, what's is going to take for my heart to love someone? If I can't love him who can I love? As I watch him drive away I quickly wipe my eyes but the tears keep coming. I try to hide them as I walk into the house but Ryan sees me crying. And runs over to me and hugs me. He brushes his hands through my hair. "What's wrong? What did he do?" he says quickly.

"Nothing. He didn't do anything." I whine.

"Then why are you crying?"

"I broke things off with him."

Ryan's POV

I know it's wrong to be so happy when she's crying but she broke things off with Christopher. She broke up with him. I have a chance, but why would she want to be with me. I realize I haven't said anything to comfort her. "Alison, it's okay. It's your first broken heart it'll get better."

"I'm not heart broken. I'm just sad because I thought he's was the guy I was going to be with forever."

"You know how I feel about that forever stuff."

"I know, but I just thought he was." Okay, maybe I was wrong about there not being that one person out there for you but I know that Alison is meant to be with the one guy that deserves her. The guy that would love her so much, take care of her and make her so happy. I knew there's was that one guy for her because if there wasn't, the rest of us wouldn't have any hope. I may not have that one girl but she does have that guy. Somewhere. "Don't worry. I know there's a guy out there for you. That guy that loves you so much and will do anything for you."

She then looks at me carefully and slowly says, "But you don't believe in that."

"I don't. But I believe in it for you. How could there not be that guy for you?" She just stares into my eyes and I break away from her stare because if I looked into her eyes any longer I'd completely lose it and just kiss her. I continued to hug her. I comforted her and held her in my arms and we stayed like that for shorter than I'd like.

CHAPTER 4

Ryan's POV

All last week Alison has been moping around the house, watching sad romance flicks while eating ice cream. She wouldn't even change out of her pajamas, she just went straight for the couch, wrapped herself up in a blanket and ate everything while she immersed herself in the cheesy love story movie. Occasionally she would shed a tear or two, but never fully cried her eyes out. Anna, our best friend, Kenny, Anna's boyfriend, and I would just stare at Alison, who was getting caught up in the romance of the movies.It was really weird how girls tried to get over a break up. I mean, why watch movies that make you more sad? I just didn't understand it. But in Alison's case, I didn't understand why she was this sad. She's the one that broke up with Christopher. Does it mean she thinks she made a mistake? Does she want him back?

Alison's POV

Just look at these two. I'm watching He's Just Not That Into You, and it's the very end of the movie where Alex goes to Gigi's apartment to profess his love for her. He just said, "You're my exception." And that was it, my eyes began to water. I wipe my eyes with tissue and suddenly the television shuts off. I look around and see Anna holding the remote in her hand. I get angry and say, "Hey! I was watching!" She looks at me in disbelief and laughs a little, "Alison! Give it up. Stop being so mopey and sad. You didn't even love the guy!" I whine, "I know... but he did mean a lot to me. And I feel like I lost someone special." She sits beside me and brushes her fingers thru my hair, "I know, but it's not the end of the world. That someone special that you're looking for is out there. You just need to stop being sad and put yourself out there. Right, Ryan?" She looks at him, hinting that he should say something, but he stays silent until I look up at him. He stumbles with his words a little, "Ye-Yeah, he's out there. I'm sure of it." Anna grabs my hand and squeezes it a little and smiles, "See! Now how about we take you to the pier today? Get some sunlight on your skin." I sigh, and get ready and put on some jeans and a t-shirt. No use saying I don't want to go, Anna will just force me, like she always does. So I make my way downstairs and see Anna with Kenny's arm wrapped securely around her waist. But where's Ryan? Isn't he going too? I don't want to be stuck with these two lovebirds, it'll just make me feel even more alone. Ryan is just sitting on the couch reading a book. Plop myself onto the seat next to him and he just looks at me confused, "What?" "Aren't you coming with us?" "Uh, no. I have something to do." "Don't give me that." I frown and whisper, "I don't want to be the third wheel" and direct my eyes towards where Anna and Kenny are hugging up on each other. A smile crept up on his lips, "Hah, no need to whisper. Besides, knowing them, they won't even notice you're there. They'll be caught up in their own lovey dovey world." "Okay, but if they're gonna be caught up in their our lovey dovey, who's gonna be there to cheer me up?" "Alison..." I pouted and he just laughed, "Fine, let's go." Once we got to the pier, I spotted multitudes of people swarming around shore. Then I saw a couple looking all cute and intimate on the sand. It wasn't gross or overtly sexual, it was adorable and you could tell they loved each other. Ryan probably saw the sadness on my face because he put his arm around my shoulder and said, "Ew, gross. Let's get out of here." He directed me towards the boardwalk. We decide to get something to eat. While Anna and Kenny went to get the food, Ryan and I went to look for tables. When we found the table and sat down. I didn't say anything because I didn't feel like talking and I think he got the hint. When I looked up from the table I saw Kenny and Anna getting cozy in the food line. Kenny had his arms around Anna's neck and he pulled her close to him as she hugged him around the waist. He just kissed her on the forehead, even though it wasn't a kiss on the lips, it was just as sweet. They love each other every much. I sigh and Ryan says, "What's wrong?" I couldn't hide how bummed out I was about not having someone to hold and hug me, "Look at them" I say a little bitterly looking towards where they were standing. "They're so cute and lovey dovey and they're just waiting in line." He smiles and laughs a little. He leans toward me to gently bump his shoulder against mine, "Jealous are we?" "Very. I mean, me being a girl and all might be a big reason why I'm jealous. But, who wouldn't want someone they can love and be with for the rest of their life?" He just looks at me and breathes in deeply. I continue, "I know you don't believe in that forever stuff, but don't you want to love someone and be loved?" He adjusted his sunglasses and looked out to the ocean and said, "I guess. I mean, it would be great to love a girl and have her love me back, but if it doesn't happen what I'm I suppose to do?" "So, you want to love?" "Of course, but if it doesn't happen. It doesn't happen. I'm not gonna live my life chasing and trying to find someone that might not even exist.""Is that the reason why you don't take relationships seriously?""Part of."Before I could ask him anything else Anna and Kenny get to the table with food. His answers totally make sense. Now I know why he is that way he is with girls and relationships. But I just wish I could've told him that he shouldn't think that there isn't someone out there for him. Of course there's a girl out there for him. Even though he's a certified "player", as most people put it, he's a great guy.

Ryan's POV

After that trip the beach, I realize that if I spend more time with Alison while she's vulnerable I might end up doing something that will ruin our friendship. So I decide to keep my distance from her so I went out with my friends tonight. I had to get out of the house because staying with Alison for any second longer would make me want her more. I had to cool off and take sometime away from her.I'm at a club, Jasmine is there with me. I have my arm around her but that's just the way I've been with her because if I didn't have my arm around her she would be all fussy and annoying. So I just saved myself from getting irritated. Jasmine starts to rub her hands up and down my thigh and she whispers in my ear, "Let's go to the bathroom. I want you." I just look at her and she grabs my hand and pulls me up and drags me to the bathroom. On the way to the bathroom I see Alison taking shots... multiple shots. She no doubt looks happy but that's because she's a happy drunk. She's with her friends but I still don't trust them enough to get her home safely. I tell Jasmine next time and walk over to Alison."Alison, what's with all the shots?" I yell over the loud music.She turns to me and hugs me, "RYAN! Nothing. I'm just having fun.""Too much fun, ey?""Not to much. Not yet. I need more shots.""Oh nooo, I know you're a happy drunk, but I know you don't want to be throwing up tomorrow.""OH come on. I don't get drunk often.""Yeah, but still. You shouldn't get drunk here, even if you're with your friends.""Anna and Kenny are here. I'll be fine.""I know they'll take care of you, but you don't want to be the third wheel do you?""OH YEAH! I forgot, I'm the third wheel." I couldn't suppress my laugh."How about I let you drink at home?""With who?" she frowned"Me." Her eyes lit up."You're gonna drink with me???" She got excited"Yeah, but only at home.""Really?""Yeah.""Promise?""Promise, but we have to go now."On the drive home, Alison just sits and starts singing along to songs on the radio, even songs she hates. She's so cute. She even starts to sway her head back and forth. When we reach home she immediately takes off her heels and jacket and grabs the liquor and brings it to the living room coffee table. She looks at me with a big smile and says, "You promised.""Yeah. I did...I don't think I should've.""But you did! So here." She hands me a shot of tequila. I down it and she just laughs."Let's play I never with shots." she says"Okay, sure.""I go first. I've never had sex""NO FAIR" I take a shot. "Okay. I've never been called a nerd.""WOW." She takes a shot "I've never had a crush on a friend."I just look at her and take a shot looking down. How did she know? She just laughs and pokes me saying, "Who did you fall for huh?" Thank God, she didn't know. But how could she not? It's so obvious. "Ryan.... Teeeelllll meee!" she grabs my arm and pulls on it."Quit it""Please? Pretty please? I'm your friend.""I'm not going to tell you, so just stop.""I promise I wont tell. Please tell me????"Then she comes closer to me leaning in. Her lips are so close to mine.

Chapter 5

Alison's POV

Leaning in was a bad idea, now I'm stuck in his gaze. He keeps looking at my lips and back to my eyes. I don't know what to do. I can't pull away, then suddenly I feel sick. Oh God, I'm gonna throw up. I run to the bathroom and Ryan runs after me and holds up my hair and rubs my back as I throw up. HOW EMBARRASSING! But at least it kept me from doing something I might regret. That was close. I felt like he was about to kiss me. I know I haven't kiss that many guys but I know that that's how Chris looked at me before he kissed me. This was weird. He was going to kiss me. Why? We are drunk, maybe that's it. I'm too weak to get up, so he carries me to my room and I tell him to leave so I can change. But once I close my door I realize I can't even unzip my dress. I call him in to help me.

Ryan's POV

I knew she drank too much. I shake my head and walk over to my room, right when I open my door she whispers, "Ryan..." Alison says shyly "Can you help me with this?"

She points to her dress. Was she serious? Does she not know that this would turn every guy on especially me, since I do like her a lot. She can't be serious. Then she looks at me with sad puppy eyes....

I'm sure it's just because she's drunk. I unzip her dress and it slips off her body she immediately puts her hands over my eyes and says while giggling, "don't look at me" She was so adorable. I turned around but then I heard her stumble over to her dresser I turned to pick her up and she said, "I said don't look" And she laughed. She got a big tshirt and put it on and her sweats. Then she started to walk to the bathroom and I said, "What are you doing?"

"I'm going to brush my teeth." When she said it, I couldn't quite understand because her words were slurred together.

"Are you sure you can do that?"

"Yeah. Why wouldn't I be able to?"

"Cuz you're piss drunk."

"Watch me."

She walks over knocking some of the stuff in the cabinet to the side and grabs her toothbrush and puts toothpaste. She begins to brush her teeth but she can barely hold herself up. She starts to lean to the right, then the left and finally she almost falls backwards but I make it to her just in time to catch her. I hold her hand to guide her toothbrush and she leans her head back on my chest and just smiles, "I swear I thought I could."

"Hahah... I bet you did."

After she rinses I guide her to her bed. I tuck her in and right before she falls asleep she says, "You will tell me who you're crushing on..."

And she fell asleep. I just stared at her sleeping. She was so beautiful and calm when she slept.

I know I shouldn't have, but I kissed her on the forehead.

Alison's POV

The next morning I woke up in my big tshirt and sweats. I remembered everything from last night. Ryan and I almost kissed but it was just the alcohol. I laughed to myself when I thought of how he helped me get dressed and brush my teeth. I must have been a handful but all he did was smile and help me. Oh that smile, it makes me melt. I go downstairs to get some breakfast and Anna and Ryan are already up. Anna just smiles at me. "what are you smiling at Anna?" I say

"Nothing." she says but giving me a 'I know something is up' look.

"What?!"

"Someone got really drunk last night."

"I know... bad, but that only happens once in a while."

"Not only that, you guys went home together."

"Yeah... we just drank here," I simply say.

"Okay.... And nothing happened?" she was still giving me the same look.

Ryan and I look at each other. And we both spit, "No."

Anna just laughs.

Ryan says, "We're just friends" and looks down.

"Fine, okay then friends. What are you up to this weekend? Because Kenny has a suite in the Wynn in Las Vegas. And I want you two to come because I feel like I haven't spent time with you two ever since Kenny and I started dating. I miss you guys." she says frowning.

I walk over to her and hug her, "Aww Anna, we miss you too. Of course we'll go."

"You had me at Vegas." Ryan says smiling.

Friday afternoon we put our stuff in the car and head to Vegas. The boys took turns driving. The first 2 hours Ryan drove and during that time I just slept. When Kenny's shift ended we stopped by a diner for an early dinner. Then It was Kenny's turn to drive. Ryan and I sat in the back seat and watched a DVD. I fell asleep on his shoulder. Once we got to the hotel, Ryan gently shook me to wake me up.

Our suite was on the 15th floor. The suite had 2 rooms with one King sized bed in each room. Anna and Kenny took one room and Ryan and I took the other. I was so excited to just go out and have fun that I didn't notice Ryan and I would be sleeping on the same bed.

That night we got ready to go out to the club. Ryan and Kenny were already waiting down stairs we just had to meet them.

Ryan's POV

While we were waiting for the girls Kenny and I went to the front desk to arrange a VIP room at the club. I was watching the basketball game on the flatscreen when I see Anna hug Kenny. Alison should be around here too. I look around and there she is, in a black sequenced strapless dress that came up just above her mid thigh. I couldn't help but smile, she was so sexy. I walked up to her and held out my hand and said, "Pretty girl, would you do the honor of being my date for tonight?"

She laughed, "Of course."

"You look lovely, Alison."

"Really? You don't think it's too much?"

"Of course, you look perfect." She smiled and blushed? I couldn't tell because of the dim lighting.

"Thanks." Once we get into the club, the crowd of people swarm around us. I hold her around the waist and squeeze through the crowd. When we get to the VIP room we all take a shot of vodka. We chat for a little bit and then Kenny and Anna start getting caught up in their own little world again. Alison gives me a "let's get out of here" look. So I ask her to dance. When we get to the dance floor, first we sway from right to left facing each other. I pull her closer to me so that our bodies are touching. She puts her hands on my chest and slowly moves them up to the back of my neck. She was looking at me smiling. I was caught up in the moment. I leaned in to kiss her but she turned her head and said, "I'm thirsty." I pull away and just look into her eyes. I had to take a second to bring myself back to reality. I really hope she didn't notice that I was going to kiss her. I let her go and we head towards the bar. I order some drinks and when I turn to look at her some guy is talking to her. She looks like she's uncomfortable. She's smiling at him just too be polite. I know her well enough to know when she's uncomfortable and this is one of those moments. When she sees me looking at her she tilts her head towards the guy hinting that he needs help. I make my way to her and wrap my arm around her waist and pull her close to me and say while looking at the guy, "You ready to go, sweetie?" I've never seen a guy look so rejected and defeated. I almost laughed out loud but I composed myself. The guy couldn't even speak so we just left. I kept my arm around her waist even after we were already outside the club. We walked around the hotel for a while looking at what else we could do but we couldn't find anything. She looked cold so I put my jacket over her shoulders as we walked. "There isn't much to do down here. I'm tired, let's just go upstairs?" she says while yawning. "You're right, let's go then?" I hold out my hand for her and she slips her hand in mine. Once we get to the suite and get to the room we get our stuff ready for bed and out of nowhere she says, "You never told me who were crushing on." I turn around and she just smiles excitedly. I turn away from her and simply say, "No, I didn't." "Oh come on! I won't tell anyone. Just tell me!." she whines."I'm not gonna tell you who. So, just give it up okay?" I say. Then it's silent for a bit and I turn to look at her and she's sitting on the bed frowning. I don't say anything and right before I go to the bathroom to shower she sighs loudly. Oh, Alison, why?I walk over to the bed and say, "Why do you want to know so bad?"She quickly recovers from her pretend sadness and brightly says, "Well, it's not everyday my Ryan has a crush on a girl. You NEVER admit to liking a girl. They're either okay and sometimes you just give them an "eh". I mean, she must be something for you to admit you have a crush on her.""Mm, she is definitely something." I say, trying to say as little as possible."Would you like to elaborate?" she gives me a knowing look"No." she frowns"You don't trust me?" she says still frowning"No, not when it comes to romance and stuff. I'm still recovering from the time you set me up with that girl in your linguistics class." I say cringing by just thinking about that date.She starts giggling, "I'm sorry! I already apologized for that. And besides, I didn't know she would be that weird."I shrug and she continues, "but anyways, can you just answer some questions? Because I can't help but be curious about this mystery woman. Who know, I could probably help you." she shoots a wink my way that just makes me smile."Fine, but only three questions and then we drop it." I say."No! How about ten?" she pokes out her bottom lip"What? How'd you go from three to ten? Uh, I'll give you five.""Seven?" she pleads."Fine.""Yay!" she happily claps. "Okay, so first question, who is she?""Haha, try again.""Fine, fine. How long have you liked her?""Uhm, I realized I liked her about 4 months ago."Her mouth forms an 'O', "What! That long? Why haven't you done anything about it?""I don't want to ruin our friendship and I don't think she feels the same way."She waits a minute before asking another question. She's thinking carefully and I'm just scared she might ask something and I might answer with something that gives it away. She collects her self and asks, "How do you know she doesn't feel the same way?" To be honest, I had no idea how to answer that question. I just said, "Um, I guess. I'm not too sure, but I'm pretty sure because if she did I would've known by now right?" "But maybe she's doing what you're doing. Maybe she doesn't want to say anything because she thinks you don't feel the same way. Okay, next, Are you just going to keep it to yourself forever?" "Uh, not forever. I mean, I'll get over it eventually. I guess." She gave me an uncertain look, "What if you don't get over it?" Then it dawns on me, what if I don't get over it? I'm going to feel this miserable forever. Oh God, if seeing her with a guy that was just her boyfriend bothered me so much, I can't even imagine how horrible I'd feel watching her get married to another guy. "I don't know." I reply looking down. "You should tell her." she said seriously. "That's not a question." I say trying to lighten the mood. "I'm serious. I mean, you don't have to do what I say, I'm no your mother. But, I think that telling her would make you feel a lot better. I can sense that this has probably been eating you up inside. What if she's that girl that you're suppose to be with?" she was looking me in the eyes now. "If she is, then it'll happen right?" She thinks for a second and says, "I guess, but, what if the only way it's could happen is if you say something? If you don't do anything and you let it pass you by, you're just gonna wonder what if? And what could've happened if you just told her." I had nothing to say. I just thought about what she said and repeated it over and over again. I was deep in thought and I looked at her and she was looking away, she was deep in thought too. Then her phone rang, she looked at the screen and she stood up and said, "Think about it" She pointed at me. She left the room and answered her phone. She said, "Hey Chris." They were talking? Before I could think of anything else, she walked back into the room. "Who was that?" I ask acting like I didn't know who was on the other line. She took out her bag of toiletries and simply said, "Oh that was Chris, we're gonna meet up on Monday." "Oh." was all I could say She went into the restroom and showered. I went to the other restroom and showered too. I finished before her so I took some pillows and settled on the couch. She got out of the bathroom and saw me on the couch. "What are you doing on the couch?" she said "You take the bed, I'll sleep here." "Don't be silly. We can share the bed. There's more than enough room. I'll build a pillow wall if you're that afraid of me coming on to you." she smiled. Oh, that wouldn't be too bad. We settled ourselves into the bed and we said our goodnights. Then she whispers, "I never thanked you for helping me get away from that guy earlier tonight. Thanks." "You're welcome. Good night Alison." "Night" she yawned "Alison?" "Mmm?" "I like you." I waited for her to say something back, but I got nothing. I sat up to look over the pillow barrier and she was sleeping already. Great.

7

Chapter 6

Alison's POV

I wake up this morning in the big king size bed feeling so refreshed and well rested. I turn over expecting to see Ryan but I'm all alone. I look at my phone to check the time and it was 9:13 AM. 'That's weird' I thought to myself. Ryan never gets up before 11AM, even when he has a class.

Ryan's POV

I didn't sleep last night. I said what I needed to say to her. She told me to tell her and I did but she was sleeping. It took a lot for me to say it out loud. Being vulnerable and telling her that I like her is something that could break our friendship. And that is not something I'm willing to lose. I can't lose her. I am so deep in thought that I hear nothing but my own thoughts. Alison waves her dainty little hands in front of my face. I look up at her and she tilts her head and smiles. She sits next to me and says, "You're up early. What are you doing down here in the lobby?""Just thinking." was all I said She bumped her shoulder against mine, "about what?""Oh no. We are not going to get into my love life again."She laughed, "Of course not. I'm just asking what you're thinking about. Geez, calm down."I heard my phone beep and took it out. It was a text from Jas inviting me to a party. I sigh and Alison gives me a questioning look. I speak, "It's Jas." It was silent for a minute. Alison turns to me and says, "Okay, I'm not trying to get you to talk about your love life again, but why are you with Jas if you like someone else." "I've been thinking about that. And maybe, I should just stay single for a while see where it gets me. Maybe it'll be good for me, you know?" I look back at her to see if I get a reaction from her. But I get nothing. She's just looking at the people passing by. She breathes, "I know you what you mean. I'm thinking about taking a break from guys. Especially like the one from last night." She laughs a little "So no guys at all?" "No. I just need time alone. I don't want to be in a relationship right now. I feel like I need a break, then maybe someone special will come along." "Yeah." We sat on the bench for a little while then headed back to the room. We left Vegas and went back to our house.

Ryan's POV

So, bad timing, but Anna leaves Alison and I at the house alone for two days. She went on a trip with her boyfriend Kenny. It's the first day and I've tried my best to stay away from Alison to keep things from happening. So far the day is almost over. I fall asleep. The next morning, I get hungry so I have to go downstairs and she's there. She smiles and playfully says, "Hey you. Why are you hiding from me?" "What?" I say back, trying to buy some time for me to come up with a good reason as to why I've been staying away from her. She walked over to the table with her bowl of oatmeal and as she sat down she said, "You stayed in your room the whole day yesterday. Whats going on? Studying?" "Yeah. I have a big test this week. I'm gonna get back to studying" with that I grab my food and head back up to my room. "Oh. Okay." I go straight to my room. Ugh, I'm really bored. I need to talk to someone. I need someone to take my mind off Alison, so I call Jasmine. She's more than happy to come over. Minutes later, the doorbell rings. I swing the door open and she smiles and says, "Hey sexy." "Hey." "I'm surprised you called. " she says as she begins to place her arms around my neck. "Yeah, me too." was all I managed to get out of my mouth "What do you want me to do?" "Come up to my room."

Alison's POV

I see Jasmine at the door. She follows Ryan up to his room. I can't help but feel... awkward. They're gonna have sex when I'm here? WHY ME? This is going to be just weird. I sit in my room hoping that I won't hear any noises so I put on my earphones and blast the music.

Ryan's POV

Jasmine doesn't waste any time. She pushes me on my bed and climbs on top of me. She starts to kiss me hard and he reaches for my belt buckle. I hold her hands and say, "Can we just do this for a while?" "What? Just make out?" "Yeah.." "Uh... why?" "I just... don't want to do this right now." "Uh okay." She starts to kiss me again. At this point I'm just laying there flat on my back, not even moving to kiss her. The only part of my body that moves is my lips. Not even my tongue is moving. She gets really impatient and starts to lift my shirt. She kisses my abdomen and moves down wards and reaches for my belt. I grab her hands again and she just looks pissed. "Ryan... what the hell?" she says loudly "Jas... I can't." "Why not?" she sounds irritated. "I just can't." "Then why did you call me here!?" "I just needed someone here." "Ugh, I'm leaving." "Are you serious? You're worst than me." "So what, we use each other for sex. That's just the way it is." She grabs her stuff and leaves. After about an hour of silence, I wonder if Alison is still home. If she isn't then

I'd be able to roam around the house and find something to do. I walk down to the kitchen and Alison isn't there. I look outside in the back yard and she's not there either. I walk back upstairs and knock on Alison's door. She doesn't answer so I open the door slowly and I see her laying on her bed with earphones in her ears.

Alison's POV

I open my eyes and see Ryan above me. I get scared and jump up."Ryan! What are you doing?" I say trying to catch my breath.He smiles and says, "I knocked on your door and your didn't answer. I thought you were dead." He sits on my bed."But I'm not. I'm here.""Haha I know that now.""Okay...""Why are you blasting your ipod?""I'm just trying to block out any sounds.""What sounds?" he says as wrinkles form above his forehead."You and Jas having sex." I whisper"What?" his eyes widen"I I thought you two were gonna have sex with me in the house." I say trying to avoid eye contact, because this was, after all, awkward."Are you serious?""Yeah...""If you did... why did you stay? Did you want to hear us?" he says while poking me with his finger.I slap him his hands away, and reply "Ew you're so gross!" He laughs. I slap him playfully and he falls backwards and rests his head on my pillow. He inhales deeply and looks up the the ceiling."I would never have sex with Jas when you're around." he sits up, turns his head to look at me and continues "I don't want you to think of me having sex with other girls.""Why?"" Just because..""What do you mean?"In a whisper he says, "I just..." and he looks at me and leans in to kiss me. His lips caught mine. At first I didn't respond but then I moved my lips with his. Our tongues massaged against each other.

Ryan's POV

She grabbed my hair and pull me closer to her. We both fall backwards and I roll on top of her. I begin to kiss her neck and down to her chest. She moans... she's wants this? I don't stop. Then suddenly we here a door slam and it's Anna, she's back. Alison pushes me off and looks frantically around. We sit on her bed and she hands me one of her ear phones and we pretend to listen to the music. Anna walks in..."Hey guys!" she chirps"Hey... how was the trip?" Alison casually says."Good good. How was being alone with out me?" Great, I thought. Then Alison said, "boring." I looked at her and she didn't look back."Okay, well I better unpack." As Anna left, we looked at each other in silence. It's like we both weren't expecting that kiss to happen, but it did. I left her room and didn't look back.

Chapter 7

Ryan's POV

As I lay in bed, I hear my alarm clock go off. I turn it off and just stare at the ceiling. Did yesterday really happen? Did Alison and I kiss? Or was it a dream? I couldn't tell reality from my dreams because the same things were happening in both. I dreamt of her all the time. The kiss couldn't have happened. I already decided that I wasn't going to act on my feelings for her because 1)When I told her I liked her, she was sleeping. She wasn't meant to hear me profess my feelings for her 2) She said herself that she wasn't ready to be in a relationship again just yet. 3) Our friendship will be ruined. Three very good reasons why I told myself I was going to keep my feelings for her a secret and why I wasn't going to do anything.I got dressed and headed down stairs. It was just me and Alison, Anna left for class. Alison just continues reading her notes. Okay, so I guess it didn't happen, because she isn't acting weird around me. When I sit down at the table I look at her again, she looks up then quickly looks back down. Oh god, it did happen. I close my eyes and say,"Alison?"She looks up first with one eye then the other. "Mmmm?""The kiss happened, didn't it?"She just stares at me"Alison ... listen-"She quickly cuts me off, "Don't worry about it.

It's okay." Then she just got up and left. This is really really killing me. I need to talk about this with her. I need to know how she feels and what she wants to do about us.

Alison's POV

Oh my god, I couldn't even look at him. I just left like a coward. He must have thought I was crazy. To tell you the truth, I don't know what to say to him. I've been thinking about that kiss ever since his lips left mine. It wasn't bad, it was actually really amazing. His lips were so soft and warm. I just was confused about why it happened. Why did he lean in and kiss me? Why did I kiss him back? We've been having weird moments staring at each other, almost kissing, but I never thought it would actually lead to a kiss. I didn't realize that there were feelings behind it, or are there? I'm sooo confused. I'm sitting in class and I don't even know what the professor is talking about. Oh no, class is over. I can't go home now. I'll have to face him. So I decide to stay in the library and study a little. It was midnight so I thought it was clear to go home. As I walk to my car I see him leaning against the driver's door. I sigh and cringe a little. I have no choice but to get in my car and leave but he was blocking the way. Once he sees me he stands up straight and nervously runs his hand through his hair. "Hey... I thought I'd find you here." he smiles a little. "What are you doing here?" "I need to talk to you." "About what?" I say innocently "You know..." "No, I don't know." "Come on! You know exactly what!" "No I don't." "Fine, I'll remind you! The kiss okay? THE KISS!" "LALALALALALALA" I cover my ears and push him aside and get into my car. I shut the door and lock it I wasn't sure what he was yelling at me but I'm pretty sure it was something along the lines of, "Are you serious? You're being so childish" I immediately backed up and rushed home. I went to my room and locked the door. I took a shower and got dressed for bed. Then I hear a knock. Knock knock knock. "Alison... I know you're in there." "go away." "I'm not going anywhere until we talk about this."

Ryan's POV

I guess I was being a little bit loud because Kenny comes out from Anna's room, "Ryan, what the hell are you yelling about?" I forgot about what time it was, "Oh shit, I'm sorry. I'll be quiet." He just shuts the door and I whisper loudly, "Alison, if you don't open the door, I'll open it myself." She doesn't say anything so I open the door using a paper clip, she quickly turns around and yells, "What the-" before she could finish what she had to say I cover her mouth with my hand and say, "Quiet. Kenny and Anna are sleeping." She was glaring at me now. I slowly release my hand from her mouth and suddenly she's slapping me. I back away with my arms trying to protect myself, "Alison, stop. Why the hell are you slapping me?" She finally stops slapping me and says, "I could've been changing!" "I already told you I was going to open the door if you didn't open it yourself." "Still!" "Whatever, stop changing the subject! Why can't we just talk about it? Stop avoiding it."

Alison's POV

"ugh leave me alone!" I say. I go to my bed and put my pillows over my ears then all of a sudden he is on top of me pulling my wrists above my head. All I could do is stare at him and he says in a firm stern voice, "We need to talk about this, okay?" I just nod. "I don't know how it happened, and I just want to know how you're feeling about everything." he said slowly. "Okay, but... I think you should let me go first" "Only if you promise not to cover your ears and say lalalala. You have to listen to me." he was serious "Okay... I promise." I breathe He slowly and gently lets go of my wrists and rolls off me. "so..." I just stay silent "Are you not going to say anything?" Still silent "Alison!" "alright! Okay... I just... I don't know what to say..." I say looking down. He just looks at me. "I mean, why did you kiss me?" "You kissed me back." he looks at me seriously I quickly retort, "But you kissed me first. You leaned in." He thinks for a moment, looks down and slowly looks up "I know I guess I was just caught up in the moment." This wasn't a statement, it was more like a question. When those last words finally left his mouth it all made sense. "That's it! I've been trying to figure out why." I mean, Ryan and I are friends. We've never felt anything close to romance towards each other. I just got out of a relationship and I guess I just missed the whole kissing thing. "So, you were just caught up in the moment? We're just friends?" he looked at me with piercing eyes. "Yeah... I mean... I guess I just miss being with someone. We're definitely just friends. " I felt relieved. Finally knowing why it happened. "Oh... I understand. But you were thinking about it aaaalllll day huh?" He was mocking me now. He was himself again. He was my friend. "SHUT UP. You kissed me!" I slapped him playfully "Haha.... Yeah.. but you kissed me back!" "What was I suppose to do? I couldn't push you off!" "oh come on. You could've said stop or kick me in the balls." "I'm just that nice." "Yeah right, you like it. You wanted me to kiss you." "Wow... big ego. Dream on. You're the one that came into my room and leaned in and kissed me." "Yeah well... now we know that we were just caught up in the moment." With that said, he gets up and winks at me. And leaves.

Ryan's POV

So she only kissed me back because she missed doing that with Chris. Maybe that's why she's talking to him again. She may not want a relationship right now because she just needs a break before she and Chris get back together. It makes sense. She did say that he was amazing and everything she wanted in a guy. Maybe now that she doesn't have him she realizes that she does love him. And now she's making it even clearer to me, "We're DEFINITELY just FRIENDS" she doesn't like me the way I like her.

9

CHAPTER 8

Alison's POV

As I lay in bed, I smile thinking about how Ryan and I joked about "the kiss". I fell asleep. But suddenly I was in the kitchen getting something to drink when Ryan comes up from behind me and grabs me. He whispers along my ear, "Alison, I want you." I couldn't believe what I was hearing, I breathed, "What?" "I need you." he breathed. I felt his breath along my neck "Ryan what are you talking about?" Then he starts kissing my lips, slowly and sensually. I give in. He then moves to my neck pulling my waist closer and closer to his body. Then he looks into my eyes and says, "You're so beautiful" Then he picks me up bridal style and carries me to his bedroom. He lays me on his bed and climbs on top of me. He starts to kiss my lips, then my jawline, then my neck, then my breasts, then my stomach. His hands reach up my shirt and grab my breasts. He takes off my shirt and his too. He unhooks my bra and starts to fondle my nipples. A light moan escapes my mouth. He smiles and then removes my pants and panties along with his pants and boxers. He kiss me again and slowly he enters me. But suddenly I wake up with uneven breaths. I'm in my bed, by myself, fully clothed. That was weird. As I sit at the breakfast table, I just stare into space. Anna starts talking to me but I'm stuck, thinking about the dream. The SEX dream. Anna tries to get my attention by snapping in my face. "HELLLOOOO! Alison!" I gasp and shake my head, "...Uh what?" Her face scrunches up as she tilts her head and asks, "What's going on with you?" "Nothing..." I sigh "Oh come on. What is it?" I bite my bottom lip contemplating on whether or not I should tell her. I mean, it's extremely embarrassing. "If I tell you, you better not tell anyone.... Promise?" She smiles and encourages me to vent, "Of course, what's going on?" "I had... a... dream." I stutter. "Okkaaaayyy?" she exaggerates the word. I look down finding a way to tell her. I stumble with my words, "It was a –a –a sex dream." I look up and she eyes widen and she shrieks, "WHAT?! With who?" "Ryan.." I whisper, looking around to make sure no one is around. "Ryan. Ryan? OUR RYAN?!?!?!" she said his name so loud, I swear I was about to slap her! I reach over the table trying to cover her loud mouth, "SHHH!" Her eyes just lit up and whisper-shouted, "I knew there was something going on between you guys!" She pointed at me accusingly. "No, there isn't!" I almost jumped out of my chair She gave me a knowing look, "then why are you dreaming of having sex with him?" She smiled like she was victorious. And she was right. She scooted closer to me and poked me on my sides, "Yeah right. Something happened between you two to make this happen." I challenged her, "Oh yeah... like what?" She was so persistent. She knew once she had me talking, I'd tell everything, "I don't know.... Something intimate. SPILL!" I gave in and whispered, "Well... we kinda kissed." She almost fell out of her chair and screamed, "What?!?!" I tried to cover her mouth again but she pushed my hands away. Once she was quiet, I continued, "Yeah... when you went away with Kenny last week" She was composed now, but now she had a curious face on. And now the questions came, "How did I not know this? And who kissed who?" "He kissed me on my bed." I admitted "And you kissed him back?" She asked raising her eyebrows "Yeah...." her jaw dropped. "Tongue?" "Yes." Her eyes lit up even more and her mouth was still open. "Grabbing?" "Yeah." "OMG you guys are in love." she held onto my wrists and shook me. "Ew, Anna shut up! We're so not" I said trying to pry myself away from her grip. "Yeah you are. This is how it all starts. You guys are gonna get married and have lots of babies" "stop it."

Ryan's POV

What the hell? She's having sex dreams about me? Does this mean she wants to be with me too? I know I shouldn't be listening but I just over heard and I couldn't stop myself, she had a sex dream about me. This is big, I'm in her mind now. Maybe fate is working in my favor this time. OH crap, they stopped talking... act natural. "Morning girls." I chime, I couldn't help but smile. "Morning." they said quickly Anna is smiling at me weird and Alison can barely look at me. I know this is awkward, but she's finally thinking about me too. This is great. I sat down to eat my breakfast and Anna leaves the kitchen. Alison gets up and for some reason all I see her wearing is a bra and panties. WHAT THE HELL???? I rub my eyes but she's still in her underwear. Now, she's walking towards me swaying her hips right to left. Oh god, she's sexy. Why is she on the table now? Oh god, Alison stop bouncing up and down. Please stop, it's too much to handle. I snap out of it and I see Alison just staring at me. "What?" I say defensively "Why are you looking at me like that?" She says slowly I look down and reply, "Like what?" "You're just looking at me weird." and she was looking at me weird too. "Oh.. I was just spacing out." I try to convince her "Oh.... Okay. I gotta go now." Okay, it's been weeks since I heard Alison tell Anna about her sex dream of us and since then I've been having sex dreams about her too. Sometimes I'd just find her in my bed, sometimes she'd be dressed up in a costume, and sometimes she's just naked. It's so distracting. I can't think about anything else. It's killing me. I can't look at her without my brain thinking about her sexually. What is wrong with me?

Alison's POV

There he is, just sitting at the breakfast table. He's always spacing out. I can't stop thinking about him naked. Not that I've ever seen a guy naked before but I still dream about it. I keep having dreams about him kissing my body, pleasuring me with his tongue just touching and teasing me. I've never had sex before and I'm dreaming about it. This isn't normal. Why can't I just forget about it?Okay, try to act normal, "Hey""Alyssa.... Hi." he was smiling at me weird again."What are you doing?" I casually askAnd he simply says, "Just thinking."I'd be lying if I said I wasn't interested in what he was thinking about. "You've been thinking a lot lately... haven't you?"He shifted slightly in his seat to face me directly "yeah... I can't stop thinking about something.""Really? Me too... it's consuming me." oh crap, I shouldn't have said that, now he's gonna want to know.He's quiet for a while and then he says, "How about you tell me what you're thinking about and I'll tell you what I'm thinking about."Hah, there is no way I'm telling him. "Uh...I can't.""Why not? We're friends right?" he says pouting his bottom lip out.Geez, he's really going to use the friend card? "Yeah...but ..."He cuts me off and says, "But nothing. You can tell me." he was grinning at me now. It's like he was just waiting for me to say something he wanted to hear."I can't...""Why not?" he pressed."Because it's embarrassing." I mumble.He smiles and keeps going, "Oh come on. I won't judge."

"No... seriously. I can't. How about you tell me what you're thinking about first?" I raise an eyebrowHe wasn't smiling now. He shook his head, "Uh... I don't know.""Wow... you wanted me to tell you first and you're not even willing to tell me first?""It's embarrassing." He laughed a little."HAHAHA... wow. Fine, then I guess we're both not saying anything."I turned my head and started to hum. I'm not telling him first.He just smiles at me and hints with his eyes telling me to go first. I just shake my head, no. SO he gives in, "Fine, I'll tell you, but you can't act differently around me."I smile knowing that I won, "Deal." we shake hands.Then he continues, "Well... I've been ... having dreams ... and day dreams.""About?" I ask"You." he says quietlyMy eyes widen in shock, "Me????""Yeah, you. Sex dreams."I could help my eyes from widening even more. I was shocked. I thought I was crazy for having sex dreams about him but he was having sex dreams about me too.After a minute of silence he says, "Soo?"I look down and mumble, "Uh... I have something to tell you.""What is it?" he says."I've been having sex dreams about you too." Slowly I look up at him and I see a small smirk forming on his lips."why are you smiling?" I was a little irritated that he was mocking me by smiling at my embarrassment. "You have sex dreams about me. And I already knew." he sang.What the hell? He did all this just to get me to admit I was having sex dreams about him. "WHAT? How?" I shriekedHe shrugged and said, "I kinda over heard you telling Anna about it."Oh man, I was sooo mad. How could he? I'm so humiliated. "OMG! How could you pretend not knowing! You jerk!" I just want to slap him"Because, I was just kinda happy and flattered that you've been dreaming about me." he was beaming as he spoke"Yeah... but you're naked in my dreams?" I don't know what face I made but it must have been the kind of face you make when you see something gross. "Judging by the way you said that, you obviously haven't seen me naked." he said arrogantly. Wow. He was really full of himself, I rolled my eyes and said, "Oh god." He sat up and made his argument, "seriously... when girls think of me naked, all they can do is smile and blush." I said, "Ew Ryan." When he said that, I felt dirty. "It's the truth." he said simply I couldn't help but ask, "But in your dreams, you've seen me naked?" He nervously brought his hand to the back of his neck and said, "...uh yeah." A light tint of red rose to his cheeks. My jaw dropped and pointed to his cheeks, "You're blushing!" "I mean, in my dreams, you're really sexy." "And in real life?" I pressed on trying to get him to admit that I was sexy. I didn't think he would actually admit it but he replied, "You're sexy." I tried to laugh it off. "haha... okay Ry." "Seriously... do you not know that?" He looks at me seriously and I'm caught in his gaze. Is it bad that I want to kiss him? Right when he leans in, the front door barges open. Our friends come in with alcohol and food. "Hey guys we're gonna play truth or dare." They ask. Ryan and I sit on opposite sides. He is still looking at me. I look down and back up but he's still looking at me.

Ryan's POV

God, why did we have to be interrupted. Now I can't stop thinking about kissing her. I need to. I can't stop looking at her. I want to hold her close. "Okay so, we're gonna go around in a circle. Taking turns." Anna says I'm right next to her and she sees me staring at Alison. She says, "Okay Ryan, you're first. I dare you to kiss Alison for 1 minute." "What?!" Alison and I manage to say the same thing. Kenny shoots her a look and she just smiles back at him and turns to me, "You heard me." I want to kiss her, but what if she doesn't want to kiss me? I'd get rejected in front of everyone. I try to get out of it,

"But..." Anna cuts me off and simply says, "No buts, neither of you and seeing anyone exclusively so there's no excuse." I just glare at her but I'm kind of happy she dared me. Alison just looks at me with big eyes, she looks scared. I want her to like it. I want her to kiss me back and like it. I get up and she walks over to me. In the middle of the circle she just looks down, then I put my hand on her cheek.

Alison's POV

He's really going to kiss me. Oh god, his hand against my skin feels so warm he leans in more looking at me straight in the eyes. His lips brush against mine. I didn't want to get carried away and he knew so he slowly pushed his lips against mine again. He coaxed my mouth open slightly with the tip of his tongue. Slowly, he moved his tongue in and out along with moving his lips. With every stroke his tongue made against mine it made me want to massage his tongue with mine too. His hand moved to the back of my neck pulling my face closer to his. Then his other hand snakes around my waist to the lower part of my back bringing my body closer to his. Right when I decide to give in, it's over. Anna says, "One minute is up." My eyes shoot open and I pull away. I manage to pull my lips away from his but he held my body close to his. He realizes we're in front of everyone. He lets go.

10

Chapter 9

Ryan's POV

After that "I dare you..." kiss earlier tonight, things have gotten worse. I can't stop thinking about her and that kiss. Okay... she was holding back but it was like it was just us and no one else around. I can't think straight I need to see her. I knock on her door.

"Come in" she chimes.

I slowly peek my head through her door "Hey..." Don't sound awkward I keep telling myself. I never had to worry about how I spoke or stood in front of her, but over the months I've become a shy, dorky and nervous guy. You know the kind, the ones that don't have the confidence to ask a girl out. Everytime I'm around her now, I just want to impress her but I do the opposite almost all the time.

"Ryan... hi." She smiles at me sweetly, it melts my heart.

"Hey, what's going on?" I say trying to sound casual.

"Nothing I'm just finishing up some homework." She was sprawled on her bed with her books and paper everywhere, wearing her huge eyeglasses. What a nerd. I went to sit right beside her on her bed as she took off her glasses.

I was unknowingly fiddling my thumbs around and when I noticed I immediately stopped and cleared my throat and said, "So our kiss tonight..."

She brought one of her hands over her faced and smiled, "Yeah... I can't believe Anna dared you." She was so cute and she didn't even try.

"yeah... me too but I am kinda of glad she did it."

Her eyebrows furrowed and she said, "What...?"

"I'm glad."

Alison's POV

What? He was glad. I was speechless. I couldn't believe it. Finally I manage to spit out, "Why are you glad?"

He just looks me in the eyes and says, "Because I've been wanting to do it for so long. Ever since you brought Chris over to introduce him to us, I realized that I really care about you and I think I might like you as more than a friend."

"Ryan, be serious."

"I'm serious." he moved closer and continued, "I've been going crazy trying to figure out why I've been thinking about you all the time, why I've been jealous, and why I've been dreaming about you. And after that kiss, I know it's because I think I'm falling for you." He looked at me with sincere, loving eyes, and stroked my cheek. He leaned in yet again and started to kiss me. This time he wasn't gentle. He pulled my whole body towards him and slowly pulled away too soon. Oh my god, his kisses are seriously to die for. No wonder why girls keep coming back. Then he said, "Alison, I want to give us a try."

"What?" I asked. I was still lightheaded from the kiss. I found myself trying to catch my breath.

"I don't want to be just friends." He tightened his grip around my waist.

"Ryan, aren't you getting a little carried away?" I whispered.

He didn't wait a second to reply, "No... We've kissed each other so many times already and it's clear that it's because we like each other."

"Actually, we've only kissed 3 times."

"So you've counted..." A smile was forming on his lips. He is so cocky.

I slapped his chest and sat up. "Shut up."

"Just kidding. I know it's a little crazy to go from being friends to possibly something more but when I'm with you I can't stop thinking about being with you."

"Ryan, we can't." I shook my head. We can't, we can't cross that line. What happens when things end badly? I'll not only lose my boyfriend but also my best friend. That can't happen.

"Why not?" he said looking a little hurt.

"We're just too different."

Ryan's POV

We're too different? What is she talking about? We have a lot of things in common.

"No, we're not"

"Yes, we are."

"How?"

"We might have a lot of things in common as friends but when it comes to relationships, we are soooo different."

"No we're not."

"Oh my goodness, yes we are! You go out with girl after girl and I'm more like a one guy type of girl."

Okay, I've had a lot of girls but doesn't she know that I would give all them up for her? Things with her are so different. I actually care about her. I might even love her. I would do anything for her.

"Okay, you're right about that, but with you things are different." Oh shit, I just sounded like every other guy on the planet. So cliche of me.

"How are things different?" she tilted her head.

"They just are." Nice answer, idiot, now she's really convinced.

"They just are." she mimicked the way I said it perfectly, except her voice was still high. I couldn't help but smile. "What does that even mean?"

"Just trust me, okay?"

"I don't know if I can."

"What can I do to prove it to you?" Anything, I'd do anything.

"Ryan, no, you don't have to do anything. It's fine, really. Kissing you has been great, believe me, but we can't be more than friends."

A smirk crept up on my lips, "Kissing me has been great?" She enjoys kissing me, something I didn't expect. I mean, I've been told I'm a good kisser, but I didn't think she would admit it to me. Especially now. I'm going to use it to my advantage.

"Is that all you got out of what I just said?" She smiled back

My eyes went to her lips, I had to steal a peck. And so I did it, I stole a quick kiss, smiled and answered, "Yeah."

She was taken aback. Then she said seriously, "Ry, we can't"

I kissed her again and still smiled, "Why not? Tell me what you want me to do to prove it to you."

She didn't expect me to do it again but she quickly recovered, "No."

I kissed her again, "Please?"

She rolled her eyes and thought for a second. Then a devilish smile formed on her lips, "Fine. Anything?"

I kissed her again and nodded.

"Then, I want you to delete all the phone numbers of the girls you've hooked up with or planned on hooking up with." She smiled like she was victorious, like she knew I wouldn't do it. But to her surprise I took out my phone, unlocked it and went to my phonebook. She looked over while I did this. I looked at her and she gave me a I-know-you-won't-do-it smile. But once I got to the delete all option, I smiled back. She didn't break her eyes from mine until she heard a click. She looked down, looked back up at me with big wide eyes and gasped, "You did not!"

It was in the process of deleting and she tried to grab my phone away from my hand, but I held it behind my back and stole a kiss from her lips again and said, "I did."

She looked worried, "Oh my goodness, Ryan! Please tell me you didn't delete your phonebook. You have stop it from deleting all of it."

I heard a beep and looked at my phone, it said 'Delete complete'. I smiled and showed her my phone and kissed her again, "Too late."

She sighed and said, "You've got to stop doing that."

I kissed her again, a little longer than before and said against her lips, "Stop doing what?"

She was looking at my lips, "That." I got her now andI couldn't help but smile.

I kissed her again. The tip of my tongue ran along her top lip and she placed her hand on the back of my neck and pulled me closer. I pulled away and said against her lips, "You want me to stop?" and continued kissing her. She pulled away and smiled against my lips,

"Yeah but like I said, I love kissing you." She pulled me towards her again and I pulled her body towards mine leaving not one centimeter between us.

Chapter 10

Alison's POV

Things were getting hot and heavy real fast. Before I knew it he was on top of me, he was kissing me along my jaw line, down my neck to just above the neck line of my blouse. I never knew making out could feel this good. Every time his lips made contact with my skin, every part of me felt like it was on fire. The way his hands massaged my hips, the way he craddled me in his arms as he placed light tender kisses along my collarbone made me want more of him. Oh. My. Goodness. This guy was incredible. His touch sent me off the edge, I wanted more, but my mind was screaming, stop, it's going to fast. And my mind was right. The pleasure he was giving me with lips, his hands sent my body on a sexual frenzy. And I knew it had to stop, "Ryan" I breathed.

"Mmm." he continued kissing my neck, which only made me moan in pleasure. Then he began to suck on the place between my neck and shoulder, it was too much for me to handle. I knew if I let me continue a second longer, I'd end up doing things I am neither emotionally nor physically prepared for.

I pulled his dark brown hair, made him face me, and said seriously, "Ryan." He was smiling at me. He knew what he was doing to me.

And once he noticed my uneven breathing, he gave me a big toothy grin. I sighed, "Ryan, this needs to stop now."

He pouted and propped himself up on his elbows, hoovering above me, and looked where he began tracing circles just below my collarbone, "but why? Didn't you just say that you love kissing me?" Then he peeked up and looked me in the eyes. I don't know if it was because I was lightheaded from our little make out session but I could've sworn I saw a twinkle in his hazel eyes.

"I do, I love kissing you, but-"

Then he cut me off, "then why does it have to stop?"

He was staring at me straight in the eyes. Why does it have to stop? We can still be friends and kiss right? We don't have to be more than that. Then it hit me, "I guess it doesn't have to." It doesn't have to mean anything.

He smiled and brushed a piece of hair away from my face, "I guess it doesn't." He leaned down to kiss me again.

In between kisses I said, "I mean, it doesn't have to be serious. We can still be just friends."

Then he suddenly pulled away and looked at me, "What?"

I tried to smile at him, "Well, you know. We can keep doing this without it having to be a big deal."

I couldn't read his expression. He just looked straight into my eyes, like he was searching for something, "You mean... friends with benefits?"

"Yeah, that's it. Friends with benefits."

Ryan's POV

Wow. I didn't expect that. Never in a million years did I expect her to suggest friends with benefits. She was under me, "Ryan, you okay?" I guess confusion and disappointment were written all over my face.

"Yeah. I'm fine. But... is that what you want?"

She answered by pulling me down to her and kissing me. "But we have to keep it a secret, okay?" I have no idea why, but I agreed. I shouldn't have but I did. Why did I do it?

She sat up gently pushed against my chest, "Alright, it's late. I have work tomorrow. I should get some sleep. And if you stay here any longer, I doubt I'll get any shut eye." She giggled. I knew what she meant by that. If it was up to me, I'd stay with her in her room for as long as I physically could.

I smiled and placed my hands on the back of her knees and pulled her into me, "Well if you have to get some sleep, then I guess I should go." She smiled and nodded.

I gave her a quick kiss on the lips and stood up and made my way to her door and she said, "I'll see you tomorrow." I turned around and saw her giving me the cutest smile I've ever seen.

"Of course, sleep tight pretty girl." She smiled even wider.

"Night Rybear." I couldn't suppress my chuckle. She came up with 'Rybear' when she tried to embarass me. She would say, "Aww Rybear!" in a tone higher than her own and pinch my cheeks. I always acted like I hated it when she called me that, but honestly I thought it was kind of cute the way she came up with a nickname for me.

I closed her door and found myself grinning like a fool.

I went to the kitchen to get a bottle of water and saw Kenny at the breakfast table busy on his laptop.

Her smile makes me melt. And when she smiles at me, I feel like it's different from the way she smiles at anyone else. And when she laughs I feel butterflies not only in my stomach but all over my my body. And those bright grey smiling eyes, just looking into them makes my day better.

"What's got you so happy?" I heard Kenny ask behind me.

I turn around and he's giving me a you're weird look, "Nothing" I chirped.

"Uh huh." was all he said and went back to working on his laptop.

I sat across from him. I was stilll smiling until the words 'Friends with benefits' popped in my head. Those three words have never made my insides cringe until now. I've been doing friends with benefits with every girl I've been with and it didn't bother me. But it can't be that way with Alison, I don't want it to be, it shouldn't be.

"Shit." I swore.

"What's wrong with you?" Kenny asked.

"I just did that stupidiest thing I could ever do." Kenny just waited for me to continue, "I agreed to be friends with benefits with Alison."

Kenny's eyes widened, "Wait. You two are?" I nodded. "You asked her to be friends with benefits?"

I groaned, "no, she asked me. And I don't know why, but I said yes."

"Alison? Friends with benefits? That's weird. Why'd you say yes?"

"I just told you. I don't know! What that fuck is wrong with me? I should've said no. Now she's never going to -"

"Dude, will you shut up for a second. Calm down." I nodded and took a deep breath. Last time I spoke to Kenny about any girl was back in freshman year and it was about Alison. After it didn't work out with Alison the first time, I gave up. And I think Kenny knew I still had a thing for her since then but he never said anything about it. Kenny isn't much of a talker, but when he gave advice it was full of wisdom.

He finished typing, then he carefully shut his laptop. He started, "So, friends with benefits huh?" Again, those three words were like daggers in my heart. I nodded "Well, I'm surprised she even suggested that. But maybe she wants it because she doesn't know what she wants with you yet."

"So what am I suppose to do? Should I take it back and tell her I can't?"

"It's up to you. You know her better than I do. But you and I both know that Alison won't do anything with you unless she felt something. And by her even bringing up friends with benefits shows that she's considering something more than friendship."

"Okay, so what? Do I just wait it out and see what happens? She wants to keep it a secret."

"Just keep showing her that you can be that guy that she's been looking for. Don't smother her, but don't give her too much space. But be careful, make sure she knows that this friends with benefits thing going on between you two is between just you two. Let her know that you're not seeing anyone else and that you wouldn't want her to see anyone else either. Give her time to realize what she feels. Because, I'm pretty sure she's feeling something. There's always been something between you guys. I just don't know why it took almost 3 years to get here." he smiled and laughed a little.

"That's a lot to remember."

"Well, if you really want her. That's the least you need to do."

"Why can't it be as easy as it was for you and Anna? Oh wait, never mind. You bitched to me, analyzing every little thing she did."

"Hey man, shut the fuck up. You're bitching to me right now."

"Now you know how it feels."

"Whatever, if you want me to keept helping you then you never tell Anna about my bitching, got it?"

"Yeah, yeah."

CHAPTER 11

Alison's POV

It's 6am, and I'm not usually this happy and excited for the day to start. I'm not saying I'm a grumpy person in the morning, but I'm almost never excited about a morning shift at Starbucks. Even though I got 4 hours of sleep, I didn't feel tired. I could've gotten 5 hours of sleep but I spent a good hour smiling and grinning at myself like a crazy person. The moment Ryan stepped out of my room, this huge smile has been permenantly plastered across my face. And I'm pretty sure when I finally got to sleep I was still smiling. I don't know what it was that kept me so happy, but I did things last night I definitely do not do. For one, I don't make out with a guy that isn't my boyfriend. It's not like Ryan's a stranger, he's my best friend so I guess that makes it better. No, actually, that makes it weird. And confusing. And.. I don't know.

I have no idea how I'm suppose to feel about all this. Ryan and I are great as friends, why would I want that to change. But oh goodness, when he kisses me my mind just stops thinking and my body takes over. That has never happened. When Chris and I kissed, I knew when it was coming and I prepared myself for it. I planned it all out. But when Ryan kisses me, it takes me by surprise mainly because I still think it's weird that we even crossed that line in our friendship. The moment his lips touch mine, almost all of my self control is out the window. I don't know what it is, but when he touches me, or even glances at me, all I want to do is be closer to him. His kisses are something I never knew I wanted it. Physical attraction is definitely there, it's always been there, but we've never gotten close enough to test it out. Now that it has happened, I don't know if I'll ever be able to restrain myself from touching him when I'm around him.

This is bad.

I've got it bad.

I went through my usual morning routine, shower, put on my black jeans, black polo, and grabbed my hat and green apron. As I turn to shut my bedroom door, my eyes rest on his door. Oh how I want to just barge in and kiss him and have him kiss me back. No. Stop right now. Control yourself, Alison. I scold myself. It took me a good minute to collect myself and force myself out the front door and walk to work. Took me about 10 minutes.

When I got to the Starbucks on campus, my coworkers Kayleigh and Timothy were already there making teas and starting up the coffee machines. I greeted them and within minutes, the line extended out the entrance. It was always busy in the mornings right before the professors and university employees had to check in for work. Once 11am hit, the amount of customers lessened considerably. Now Anna's shift began while Tim's ended.

When there was no line, I went to refill the sugar and straws at the island and then the bell on the door rang. I looked towards the entrance and saw Anna hand in hand with her boyfriend Kenny. And following a few feet behind was Ryan. He was dressed in just dark blue fitted jeans and a simple grey hoodie. He looked so cute and always handsome. That smile from earlier this morning slowly disappeared when work got busy but somehow I knew that that smile was nothing compared to the one I had now. I tried to direct my attention to the happy couple holding hands, "You really made him drive you when it's only a ten minute walk?" I teased Anna.

"I didn't make him, he wanted to get something to drink!" she tried to defend herself and she turned to Kenny as he said, "She's right. I wanted to get some coffee before I leave for LA" Then, being the charming lady she is, Anna stuck her tongue out at me playfully.

Then I heard a voice from behind me, "You know, I could've taken you to work this morning. You should've woken me up" Ryan smiled and his eyes danced between my lips and eyes.

"Don't be silly. I know how much you love your sleep." I teased him and smiled. But a hint of sadness was in his eyes. "Besides, I love the morning walk. It wakes me up."

Before he could say anything else, Kenny already had his drink in his hand. He said goodbye to Anna and hugged her tightly and gave her a quick kiss on the lips. He walked over to me, "Alison, I'll see you in a few days. Make sure Anna doesn't go crazy with the online shopping?" I giggled. Anna really did love shopping, especially online shopping since she could do it anytime she wanted. He gave me a hug and I guess he was going to give Ryan a ride back. Wait. Why did Ryan come here? Just to see me? I thought. Ryan awkwardly said goodbye to me. But when he and Kenny were at the door it looked like they were arguing over something. Ryan nervously rubbed the back of his neck and turned to face me as he walked back to me. Why is he acting so weird?

Finally he stopped in front of me. I waited for him to speak but he just smiled nervously and avoided eye contact. He was being awkward which made me awkward. Ugh. What is happening?

"So..." he started. I just stood there with straws in both my hands. I looked at Anna and she just gave me a questioning look. I looked back at him and he continued, "maybe, I could pick you up later?"

Was that all? "You don't have to. I get off at 2."

He spoke up immediately, "No. I want to. I'll be here a little earlier than that. Is that okay?"

"Okay, sure. I guess."

He exhaled like he was relieved, "Okay. Great. I'll see you later."

It looked like he was going to give me a hug but then he stopped when he saw the straws in between us. He smiled and said, "Bye."

He walked away and I saw Collin. "COLLIN! Are you working today???"

Ryan curiously eyed Collin, but I'm sure it was nothing.

About an hour later, Starbucks was desserted. We had nothing to do so we just chatted while we cleaned up. While I wiped the tables, I unknowingly started to hum and think about the night before.

"Someone's happy." I heard Anna say. I looked over at her and she was smiling.

"Who me?" I asked looking to where she was, with Kayleigh and Collin smirking at me.

"Mhmm. Girl, who are you thinking about?" Kayleigh asks. I was thinking about Ryan but I can't say anything. Him and I are just friends, nothing more can come of that.

"Was it that delicious looking guy you were talking to earlier?" Collin said wiggling his eyebrows. Sometimes I forgot that Collin was gay because of his deep voice and his handsome features. I know that not all gay men are suppose to dress or speak girly but when it's not obvious I don't catch on that quickly. And when he makes comments like that, I am fully aware of how gay he is. Collin has never been one to hide his feelings. He says what he wants when he wants. He speaks more about guys than I do.

I couldn't hide my smile, "Ryan? We're just friends."

"Hmm, that cutie has such a cute name." Collin cooed

Kayleigh laughed, "I think you're as gay as it gets." Collin playfully poked her sides and Kayleigh squirmed.

"So this Ryan, how do you know him?" Collin asked.

Kayleigh answered for me, "She just told you, they're just friends" She put just friends in air quotes, "Which I have no idea why you're just friends. He's such a stud. You live in the same house for God's sake, how can you still be just friends?"

"Oh my god, you live with that sexy god? How? Have you seen him naked? Oh I know what I would do if I lived in the same house with him." Collin said and I giggled. He really is as gay as it gets.

"Collin, keep it in your pants. Geez" Anna teased and Collin just laughed. He didn't mind when we teased him about his forwardness or his gayness. "Ryan use to be Kenny's roomate freshman year, they were suppose to live together for sophmore year but Kenny left school to launch his business. Ryan couldn't find a place to live because it was too late and Alison and I needed a roomate so we just decided that he should live with us since we were all already good friends." Anna shrugged.

Collin's mouth was open, "OHMYGOD, so you've been living together for almost 2 years and neither of you have gotten on that???" I giggled and rolled my eyes. Collin seriously needs a boyfriend. Not that he can't get one, but I could sense he wants one. Then he continued, "I mean, I know why Anna hasn't tapped that. But you." he pointed to me, "Alison, honey if you don't claim him now, I'll have to make a move myself."

"No, I will. Ryan's not gay, Collin. He likes girls. Lots of girls, in fact." Kayleigh responded, "Wait. Is he seeing anyone right now? Ughhh, why can't I hook up with him again?"

The thought of Ryan and Kayleigh "hooking up" made my insides cringe. I didn't like that at all.

"Because, Kay, it's a rule. He can't date our friends remember? When he starts seeing a girl they break up and the girl is always hung up on him. It makes things weird for us" I said but that wasn't the only reason. I don't want them to hook up. Ever.

"Oh yeah. Stupid rule." she sighed.

Anna laughed, "Alison and I need to find you and Collin boyfriends. Which reminds me. Plenty of cute available guys will be at my birthday party next week. You two better be there." Both Kayleigh and Collin nodded and danced in delight. "But, remember, Ryan is OFF LIMITS." Then she shoots me a look and winks at me.

I roll my eyes. Sometimes I wish she didn't know me so well. Right then, she was probably plotting some scheme to get Ryan and I together.

Before I knew it, it was 2 o'clock. Ryan was early like he said he would be.

Ryan's POV

I'm waiting outside Starbucks and I see Alison walking towards the door. As she opens the door she says, "Collin, we better get the same shifts. I missed working with you." She laughed and pushed the door further open, "Bye Anna see you at home. Later Kay."

Who's this Collin guy? She looked awfully happy to see him earlier and now she was saying that she wanted to work with him more.

She turned towards me and smiled big, "Hey!" She hugged me around my middle and I wrapped my arms around her.

Oh shit, not again. Why do I get all nervous and fidgety when I see her now? Be cool, Ryan. Be cool. "Hey you, how was work?"

She let out a sigh as she removed her hat and apron, "Oh my goodness, this morning was so busy! I spilled white chocolate mocha on my pants, and caramel got all over my shoes." She looked up at me and frowned. She's so adorable.

I just smiled and opened her door, "Aww. It's okay, you still look cute."

She wrinkled her nose, "Hardly. I probably have caramel stuck somewhere on my face or in my hair."

I stepped closer to her and gently held her chin in my hand and pretended to inspect her face, "Mm, nope, no caramel anywhere. All I see is the prettiest face."

A light shade of pink rose to her cheeks, "Right."she said sounding unconvinced.

She slipped into the passenger seat and the ride home wasn't too bad. But I have to find a way not to get nervous. If I see her after not seeing her for an hour or more, I get really nervous and forget everything I want to say and do. But somehow, she finds a way to make me relax. Maybe it's her smile, or the way she laughs, or the way she wrinkles her nose when I say something absurd, or her laugh. Maybe it's everything about her. I really have no clue. All I know is that whenever I'm around her I feel everything good, exciting, wonderful.

Once we got into the house it was awkward again. It was silent. We looked at each other for a bit, then looked away, then we both started, "So..." Ugh, why am I such a loser? I can't even talk to her, how am I suppose to make her fall in love with me? I thought she would show some expression of annoyance or irritation but she just giggled and smiled at me.

"Ryan, what's going on with you? Why are you being so weird?" she tilted her head.

I sighed, "I honestly have no idea. I'm trying to act normal and be normal but I just end up being awkward."

Then she frowned, "I knew this would happen, you and I don't make sense together. This is why I didn't want us to be more than friends. It's all weird and awkward for us both. We were fine as just friends, now look what's happened. We can't even be ourselves around each other anymore."

"Alison, no. The only reason why it's awkward is because I have no idea how to be around you. Especially in public. You want me to keep this a secret and I have no idea how to do that with you."

"You of all people know how friends with benefits works." she started. Oh, those three dreadful words, I suddenly felt a pang in my stomach. "That's all you've done with the girls you've been involved with."

"Yeah, but it's you. I can't just treat you like I did the other girls. I actually care about you, you're my best friend, Alison. None of those girls knew me like you know me. They got to know a guy completely different from the guy you know. But you. You know everything about me, how I am." She just stared at me. "And us, you and me, we do make sense. I would've never told you how I felt unless I knew you and I could really work. I would never jeopardize our friendship just to see if we would work out. I know we could work."

She looked at me with a slight smile on her face and just like that, everything fell into place for me. I knew I wasn't going to be nervous anymore. That small smile she gave me gave me hope that she could possibly see a future with me too. That's all I needed. I just needed to know that I had a chance. Her eyes met mine, those bright smiling eyes were twinkling. I reached my hand up to her face and I slowly brought my face closer to hers and before our lips met she spoke, "I smell like coffee."

I smiled, "I don't care" and kissed her.

The next 3 hours were spent in her room, on her bed. Our legs were tangled up, my arms wrapped securely around her waist. Her hands clutched my hair. The time went by so quickly, I guess she forgot that she and Anna were suppose to go shopping at 5:30. We were interrupted by a knock on the door, "Alison, you in there?"

Alison pushed me off her and one of our phones hit the ground with a loud thump. We heard the door knob twist but it was locked, "Alison, I know you're in there. Let's go! You said you'd be ready."

Alison looked around her and her eyes finally landed on her closet. She got up and pulled me by the wrist to her closet. "Stay in here, " she whispered.

Before she could close the closet door, I couldn't resist the urge to pull her close for a another kiss. I pulled her waist towards me and I kissed her. She quietly moaned. "Alison, seriously. What are you doing in there? We have to go."

She whispered with a smile on her face, "Ryan, I have to get that." She had to pry my arms off her and she closed her closet.

I heard the door open, "Anna, can you give me a sec?"

"Yeah, fine. But only 5 minutes alright?" Then there was a pause, "Are you alright? Why are your lips swollen?"

I couldn't suppress my laugh, I guess it was a little too loud because Alison coughed to cover up my laugh, "Um, I-I don't know. Maybe it was the new chapstick I used, it probably had some pomegranate stuff it in. You know I'm allergic."

"Sure." Anna said unsounding unconvinced. "5 minutes! I'll be back."

I heard a door close and lock. Then footsteps until it stopped in front of the closet doors. Alison opened it quickly. She was glaring at me but also trying to hide a smile, "You're really bad at keeping quiet. This is suppose to be a secret remember?"

She was standing in front of me with her hands resting on her hips. She looked so cute pretending to be angry with me, I couldn't help but smile. I stepped closer to her and slipped my arms under hers and linked my hands at the small of her back, "Well, you're a really bad liar. Pomegranate stuff?" I teased.

She still kept her hands on her hips and stuck her tongue up at me, "Hey! You try lying to your best friend. And besides, I'm pretty sure I could've stayed quiet if I was the one in the closet."

I raised my eyebrows, "Oh really?" She nodded with a grin. I pulled her into the closet and shut the closet doors.

She giggled, "What are you doing?" I felt her hands run up my arms to my shoulders till she finally made it to the back of my neck.

I tightened my grip around her waist and leaned my head down till our lips were touching, "Let's see if you can keep quiet."

She giggled again and I captured her lips with mine.

Eventually, we made our way out of the closet. She left with Anna and I waited to leave her room until they were finally gone.

CHAPTER 12

Alison's POV

"Ohmygod! That's the one! You have to get it!" Anna squealed as she looked over my dress. I don't even know why I was buying a new dress since it's her birthday party to begin with. But Anna always insists on me joining in on her let's-try-on-everything-in-the-store game. I've only known her for almost 3 years and I've learned more about fashion in those 3 years than I have my entire life. I wasn't by any means a fashion disaster but I wasn't exactly on my way to walk the runway. Never the less, my impeccable fashion sense is all thanks to her. I walked over to the full length mirror to get a glimpse at this dress that I have to get. I looked at myself. It was a short blue and black mini dress that came up above mid thigh. It did wonders for my small and short frame. It made my legs look longer and slimmer. It was definitely a good find.

Kayleigh walked out of the fitting room wearing a emerald green minidress. She looked gorgeous. She was taller than me, her legs went on for miles, she looked like a model. "Holy shit Alison, where have you been hiding that sexy little body"

"Seriously, Alison. Damn, we're going to turn some heads Friday night. Not that care, I have a boyfriend. But you two are definitely getting some" Anna said as she walked over to the mirror in her pink mini dress. Anna was a little bit taller than I was, andI envied those gorgeous curves shehad. She knew exactly what to wear to showcase her assets and that mini dress did wonders for her alreadysexy body.Yes, we were all wearing mini dresses, but each had there own flare to it.

As I tried to unzip my dress, I heard my phone beep. It was text. As I've done millions of times over the course of our friendship I asked Anna to check it for me, but this time I should've just let it gone unchecked. Anna reached in my Marc Jacobs purse and took out my iPhone and punched in my password. "Oh. My. God." she said slowly but clearly.

I looked up at her confused, "What?"

"Text from Ryan."Oh no,I groaned inwardly. "Hurry home, pretty girl. I miss you xxx" She read in a deep voice to sound like Ryan. I froze. I didn't know what to say or do. I felt my cheeks grow warm. Not because I was embarrassed or because I felt like a criminal that just got caught but because it just made what Ryan and I have even more real to me. If that even makes sense. Since we started our little friends with benefits thing, it always felt like I was living a fantasy or dream because no one knew except for me and him.

"Holy crap! You and Ryan are doing the nasty!" she teased. Always leave it up to Anna to make an already awkward situation even more awkward. The nasty... who calls it that? If I wasn't blushing before, I'm definitely am now.

I rolled my eyes trying to play it cool, "We are not."

"So then what?" she raised her eyebrows, "What are you two doing?"

"Nothing" I said innocently

She shot me a knowing look, "Look, I know you never really like talking about relationships and stuff, but be real with me. Are you two having hot, steamy sex under our roof, young lady?"

Kayleigh laughed, "So does this mean he's off the market now?"

"He's always been off the market because his heart belongs to Alison" she sang "Alison and Ryan sitting in a tree K-I-S-S-I-N-G, first comes love, then comes marriage, then comes the baby in the baby carriage."

Kayleigh was seriously amused. She was basically rolling on the floor laughing gasping for air. I know this seems like torture, but it wasn't. Anna knows that I can take a joke. I don't mind. I actually found myself giggling a little when she sang that song.

"Okay I'm done with the teasing." Anna managed to say with a serious but interested tone, "But what's really going on?"

"Well, we're kind of doing the whole friends with benefits thing." I said quietly.

Suddenly Kayleigh wasn't laughing anymore, "Whoa."

"What?" I said defensively

"Nothing, it's just. You're not really the type of girl that does friends with benefits. I mean you're sweet, adorable Alison."

"What's that suppose to mean?" I say irritated.

Anna holds up her hand to speak, "What Kay is trying to say is that you're the type of girl that guys want to be with forever. You know, the girl that they need. The girl that, once they realize that they need to settle down, they can be in an actual relationship with. Friends with benefits is a game, and you're not the type of girl that deserves to get played around with."

"But what if I just want to have fun? I don't want to have to worry about it meaning anything."

"Oh honey, it always ends up meaning something to someone whether you want it to or not. It's a dangerous game and someone always gets hurt." She looks at me seriously and added, "I'm not trying to make you feel sad or discouraged but I'm just telling you the truth. I don't want either of you to get hurt. Just think about it, okay?"

I nod and we stop talking till we're out of the store. We say our goodbyes to Kay and then drive home.

On the drive home my thoughts are running a million miles per second. Someone always gets hurt. Someone always gets hurt. Someone always gets hurt. I don't know what scared me most, me getting hurt or him but I knew that if either one of us did get hurt our friendship was over. The thought of us not speaking or seeing each other frightened everything in me. Not being able to hear his laugh, not being able to see his perfect smile, not being able to feel his arms around me would be a living nightmare. What am I getting myself into? How could I ask him to do this, whatever we were doing, with me?

Once we walked through the front door we saw Ryan sitting in the living room surfing the web on his laptop. He looked up at us with a dashing smile, "You're home."

"Yup" Anna smiled uncomfortably and started walking up the stairs, "I'll leave you two to talk."

He eyed me curiously.

"She knows." I didn't have to explain, he knew what I was talking about. His smile grew wider as he walked towards me and scooped me up in his arms.

He leaned in to give me a kiss but once he saw the expression on my face he frowned and set me down, "What's wrong? Are you mad that she knows? Because I kind of told Kenny already. I'm sorry."

I shook my head and sat on the couch, he sat beside me and whispered, "Then what's wrong?" He swept a piece of my hair behind my hair to look at me better.

I looked up from my hand into his eyes, "Are we doing the right thing? Us. I mean." He stiffened beside me and swallowed hard. "We're having fun right?"

"Of course. I'm having fun, aren't you? I know what I want for us, you know what I want. I just don't think you know what you want." I turned my head down once again. He was right, I don't know what I want. I really want to want him but how can I when there's a possibility that things could end badly. That our friendship could end. "Hey, look at me" he gently lifted my chin so that I could see him, "Don't feel obligated to be with me. There's no pressure. I don't want you to be with me because you think that it'll hurt my feelings if you don't. Sure, it'll hurt if you don't feel the same way and want to stop, but I'd rather be hurt than make you do something that you don't want to do. I want you to want to be with me. And I'll give you as much time as you need to figure it out, okay?"

"Okay." I breathed and he wrapped his strong arms around me as I rest my chin on his shoulder.

"You don't need to worry." he whispered into my hair. How could I not worry? Going into this, I thought it would just be all about fun. Sneaking around, tight embraces, lots of stolen kisses here and there. I didn't think everything would get so intense so fast. We weren't even dating and everything felt like so much.

Someone always gets hurt. Someone always gets hurt. Someone always gets hurt.

CHAPTER 13

Ryan's POV

"Man, what the fuck? You had him!" Kenny yelled as he focused on the flat screen. We were playing gears of war on my Xbox. Usually I'm into the game kicking Locust ass but right now I can barely think. Alison has been distant with me this past week. Ever since she came home asking me if what we were doing was right she's been pulling away from me. I didn't say anything about it because I didn't want her to finally decide that I wasn't what she wanted, and realize that I don't deserve her. Even though I have a feeling that this could be the end of us I wasn't going to stop proving to her that I could be that guy for her. It's her decision, and I was going to do everything to get her to choose me.

I didn't respond. I was frustrated. Frustrated that I couldn't get my head together to beat the Locust. Frustrated that things between Alison and I were rocky and unstable. Just plain frustrated. So I just pounded the keys on my controller until I died again leaving Kenny to fend for himself. I sat back in defeat and watched Kenny get torn apart till it was a failed mission. We both threw the controllers to the rug.

"What the fuck man? We were so close! You're better than me, how in the world did you die first?" I know it sounds like Kenny was way to into the game but that's just how guys are. When we're in the zone, there's absolutely no going back.

"It's over" I sighed.

"Yeah, I know dumbass, you left me to die." he chuckled

"No, I mean. We're over." I sighed again.

Kenny looks at me confused "What are you talking about?"

I set my head back on the couch and looked up towards the ceiling, "Dude, I think she's going to break up with me. Not that we were together in the first place, but you know what I mean."

"I thought things were good between you two? When I left, you were smiling like an idiot. I gave you advice. Did you not use it?"

I sit up and say, "I did! I did exactly what you said to do. I'm trying to show her that I can be that guy for her. I have no idea what I'm doing wrong but last week she asked me if what we were doing was right."

"What did you say?"

"I told her that I know it's right because I want us together, but I don't think she knows what she wants. She didn't say that she wanted to stop being with me, but lately she's been holding back."

"Maybe it's time you make it absolutely clear that you want to be with her. Officially. And ask her if she wants the same thing too."

"I don't think I can do that."

"Why not?"

"Because, what if she doesn't want the same thing? What if she doesn't feel the same way? Honestly, I'm perfectly okay with just having her with me the way we are now than not having her at all.

Even if she's not sure about how she feels, and unsure about what she wants. I'd be okay with that even if it's killing me"

"Man, you got it bad." He said as he pat me on the back.

Yes, I do.

Alison's POV

"God, can someone get this girl a drink? Cause she sure looks like she can use one." Collin said as he eyed me from behind the counter. "What's got you all sad looking?"

"It's nothing." I sighed.

He rolled his eyes and sat across from me at the table, "It's never nothing. And when I see you, happy giggly Alison, frowning something must be wrong. If you were someone else I'd tell you to suck it up, but it's you. I have a soft spot for you in my gay little heart. So spill."

And so I did. I spilled. I told him basically everything Anna, Kayleigh and I discussed while shopping. He listened intently and took in every detail. This is what I loved about Collin, I don't know if it's because he's gay, but he listened like a girlfriend would listen. He looked at me and nodded. His eyes were sincere and looked as if he was feeling what I was feeling.

"So now I don't know what to do." I say

"What do you want to do? It's not about knowing what to do. First, it's all about what you want. When you know that then you'll know what to do. So, what do you want?" he asked.

"I don't know." I said honestly.

He shook his head and smiled a little, "Stop thinking. I can tell you've been racking your brain about this for some time now. Don't think about what might happen in the future. Don't think about how he feels. Don't think about anything. What do you want?"

Without thinking I said, "I want to be with him."

He smiled warmly, "Okay, now how do you feel about him?" As I opened my mouth to speak but he continued, "Oh wait. Let me ask this cause I know you're going to say you don't know. How would you feel if you saw him with some girl, let's say Kayleigh, making out?"

I winced. I didn't want to picture that. I was already getting jealous just thinking about it. "I'd feel horrible."

Collin's smiled exploded into a full on toothy grin, "I think you know what to do now."

"But. But what if things end badly?" I sad slowly and quietly

Collin's smile turned into a sincere thoughtful smile, "Someone once told me to stop being afraid of what could go wrong and think of what could go right."

I smiled. At that moment I knew. I knew what I wanted. I wanted Ryan. Not as my friend, not as my friend with benefits. I wanted him right beside me always, as more than a friend. I stood up straight and walked towards the door to leave.

"Where are you going, silly? We don't get off until 9." Opps. I totally forgot. I was so wrapped up in my emotions that I was just about ready to drop everything and tell Ryan how I felt. Collin saw how embarrassed I was and walked over to me and gave me a kiss on the forehead, "Patience, my dear. You'll get to him."

By the time 9pm rolled around I was already out the door and walking back to the house. When I got there, I immediately ran up to his room. I knocked. Once, twice. Then knocked again until I realized that no one was home. Anna and Kenny were already at the club and Ryan was probably there too. So I got ready. I showered, slipped into my black and blue minidress, fixed my hair into soft curls, applied some makeup, and put on my black pumps. I took a long look at myself on the full length mirror. I looked good. Sexy even. I smiled. Tonight was the night. I'm scared and nervous, but I'm so very excited and happy that I finally knew what I wanted. I'm ready.

Collin picked me up from the house and we arrived at the club together. He could sense that I was nervous as we walked through the front doors of the club.

He put his arm around my shoulder and pulled me into a side hug, "You can do this" he said with an encouraging smile.

I took a deep breath and nodded. I can do this. I can do this. I smiled back up at him, "Thanks Collin. For everything."

He kissed my forehead, "No problem, hun. Now lets go." He took my hand in his and we made our way to the group.

Every step we took made my heart beat accelerate. The music blasting off the walls was nothing compared the thump thump thump sounds my heart made. I was no longer nervous, just plain excited. I was practically skipping to the group, pulling Collin along with me.

"Ally babe! Collin!" Anna squealed "You're finally here!" She pulled me into a tight hug. She was tipsy but very happy. She had a big smile that was contagious. And she had her boyfriend, Kenny, smiling at her adoringly. Now, I just wanted to see Ryan. "Come! Let's take a shot! To my favorite coworkers, thank you so much for making it to my 22nd." Kayleigh and Timothy joined us and we clinked our shot glasses together and drank.

Then, Kenny gathered everyone to take a shot and toast to the birthday girl, "Everyone raise a glass to the most beautiful, vivacious, brilliant woman in the room. Anna, babe, I love you. Happy birthday, dear." She wrinkled her nose, smiled and stood on her tip toes to kiss him. "To Anna." We toasted and drank, again. Just looking at Anna and Kenny embrace each other made me want to find Ryan. I need to find him and tell him. Now.

I look around. It's really hard to see, it's dark with dim lighting and the flckering strobe lights weren't helping. I saw lots of familiar faces. I should've said hi but instead I just smiled and waved because all I wanted was to find Ryan. I was beginning to get worried. Even though I knew he was there, every second that passed without me seeing him sucked. Then, I saw him. He was dressed in a simple button up shirt rolled up at the sleeves and dark washed jeans. He looked gorgeous. He was chatting with a girl while sipping on a beer. He looked my way and our eyes met. I smiled at him and all he gave me was a weak smile and turned back to the girl he was speaking to. Am I missing something? What just happened? I waited for him to look at me again, but he didn't. My heart just... sank. I stood there looking at the pair talking and when I looked closely I found out that the girl was Jasmine. Tall, skinny, big boob Jasmine. Of course. They have a history of hooking up. Jealousy was boiling inside of me. But I had no right to be jealous, and even if I did there was nothing to be jealous of, right? They're just talking. Nothing serious. Maybe I should tell him after the party.

Right when I turn the opposite direction I run into Collin's chest. I look up at him, "Whoa, where are you going? He's that way." he said pointing behind me.

"Um, I just going to get a drink first." He shook me a knowing look. "Just one drink. I promise. Then I'll talk to him."

"Mhm."

One drink turned into four and I just kept making up excuses for not telling him. I sat there and watched Ryan and Jasmine talk and talk.

"Ally babe! What are you doing here all by yourself?" Anna slurred.

"Nothing."

She squinted her eyes turned to where I was looking. "They're just talking, you know."

"Here babe. Just water for now, okay?" Kenny said taking a seat next to my best friend.

"Honey, tell her she has nothing to worry about. Ryan's just talking with Jasmine." Anna murmured.

Kenny looked confused for a second then looked at Ryan and Jasmine. "You're crazy if you think he's interested in her." he said to me.

"Well, they did have sex. And lots of it." I said bitterly.

Kenny chuckled, "Just because they had sex doesn't mean he cares about her. He doesn't look at her the way he looks at you. That guy is crazy about you and if you feel the same way go get him."

"I don't want to interrupt."

"Yes you do. And he wants you to interrupt too, believe me. Go get him."

Ryan's POV

Jasmine. She's going on and on about God knows what. Thirty minutes of pretending to be interested. I'd rather shoot myself but this will have to do. I wasn't about to approach Alison and that Collin guy. First I see him kiss her forehead when I was about to surprise her at work, then they arrive together looking like they match, then he kisses her forehead again, and finally they hold hands. I know

Alison and I never established that we weren't going to see other people but I thought that went without saying. And I never thought she would do that to me. I mean, I'm not just some guy, I'm her best friend. I thought she care about me that much but I guess not. She made her decision about who and what she wants. She wants that Collin guy, not me. I wish she could've just told me instead of making me look stupid. So I just decided to stay away from her as much as possible. I don't want to see her and Collin holding hands. I don't want to see him giving her kisses.

Alison appears out of nowhere, "Hey Jas. Ryan." she said looking me in the eyes.

This is the closest we've been all night. She's within arms reach. I can already smell her sweet smelling perfume. She's more radiant up close. She looked hot at the club entrance, but I didn't know she looked this sexy. Her dress was hugging her in all the right places. Her legs long and lean, her hips perfect, her stomach flat, her waist tiny. That dress was tiny, the hem was above mid thigh, and she was showing way more cleavage than I'd like. Guys were oogling her breasts and ass. I didn't like it. And God that beautiful face. Her pink plump pouty lips glistened. I don't what it is... gloss? They looked delicious, I wanted a taste. Her cheeks were naturally rosy and her nose was perfectly small and pointed at the end. And those grey eyes, were so stunningly bright. Her hair looked so shiny and soft. It was long and curly tonight. Her neck was long, her shoulders and collarbone were exposed because her dress was strapless. I just wanted to nuzzle my face into her neck and plant sweet gentle kisses all over her. Her skin was glowing, I needed to touch.

"Hi" I managed to say without breaking eye contact.

A moment passed before Jasmine tried to get my attention back on her, even though she never really had it, "So, as I was saying, we should go right?" I had no idea what she was talking about.

"I'm sorry, but, Ryan, would you like to dance with me?" Without being rude, Alison politely diverted the conversation back to me and her. I loved that about her. She didn't have to be rude to get her point across. She was always polite and sweet.

Without looking at Jasmine I excused myself and took Alison's hand and led her to a place that was semisecluded. She gently placed her hands on my shoulders and my arms wrapped around her waist. Because it was a club, the music was fast and the beat was nowhere near a song you can slow dance to, but we didn't care. We just swayed together. Our eyes were still locked together.

She leaned in closer so I could hear her, "So. I haven't seen you all night." she slowly slid her hands to the back of my neck, playing with my hair.

I leaned towards her ear and held her close, "You seemed preoccupied with Collin so I thought I'd just give you guys some space."

She pulled away slightly to look at me and cocked her head to the side with a smile, "Why would you do that?"

"Because, I thought you'd want time with him since you like him and he seems to like you too."

She smiled sweetly, "We're just friends."

"It's fine. You're interested in him. I get it."

She giggled, "What? It's not like that. Collin's gay."

"He's- He's what?" Oh thank God.

Her smile widened, "Gay."

"Wow."

"Is that why you stayed away from me all night?" I nodded and she tip toed and pulled me closer to her. I felt her lips brush against my ear, "You should know by now that you're the only guy I'm interested in."

I squeezed her sizes and finally let out a smile, "Really?"

She nodded and her face softened, "I'm sorry for being weird and being distant lately. It's just that I've been worrying about what would happen if things between us ended badly. I don't ever want us to stop speaking. I want you in my life always. You're my best friend and I care about you a lot." I nodded, I felt the same but I wanted more. "But I'm scared. Scared of all these strong feelings I ave for you. Everything is moving so fast between us. It's all so intense. And I thought that it would be better if we just stayed friends but I don't think I can just be your friend. What I feel for you is so strong, so intense. I'm falling so hard and so fast and it scares the crap out of me but no matter how scared and unsure I am I know that I want to be with you. I want to give us a try. Officially. But only if you still want to."

Her eyes were piercing through mine. Almost like she's pleading. But does she not realize that this is what I've wanted for so long.

"Of course I still want to."

Before I knew it, her lips were on mine. It's not that I didn't like it... I loved it. She surprised me and when I finally realized what was happening I kissed her back with everything in me. This gorgeous girl wants to be with me. Everything is finally how it should be and I couldn't be happier.

CHAPTER 14

Alison's POV

My head was pounding. I. Need. Aspirin. I thought to myself. I felt an arm around my waist. And for a moment I couldn't remember what happened the night before. I wasn't in my dress. I don't remember changing. I freaked out and flipped around and my hand accidentally hit a guy's face. Ryan's face.

"Ow" he groaned and placed his hand over his right eye.

"Oh crap. I'm sorry! I didn't mean to hit you!" I sat up, gently cupped his face in my hands and tried to see if his eye was hurt. He squinted his eyes and tried to adjust his vision by blinking. I felt bad for hurting him but he wasn't supposed to be in my bed. "Why are you in my bed anyways?"

He blinked a couple of times and rubbed his eyes. Once he registered what I just asked him he chuckled and said "What do you mean why am I in your bed? You kind of begged me to stay with you."

"Oh" I felt my cheeks grow warm. I knew I was blushing like crazy because of the big grin on his face. I'm never usually that forward. I tried to remember what happened last night, but most of it was a blur.

He looked at me while I tried to replay last night in my head. Last thing I remember is Kenny practically carrying a giggling Anna in his arms out of the club. "Please tell me you remember what you told me at the club."

He looked at me with worried eyes. He was worried that I couldn't remember telling him that I wanted to be with him. But I remember what I said and the fact that he was worried was cute. "Of course I remember." I smiled warmly to reassure him of what I said.

His face brightened, "So it's a official? You and me?" I nodded and his hands gently pulled me by the hips closer to him. Every time he touched me softly like he was just then my heart felt like it was doing back flips. When he was with other girls before me, like Jasmine, he would usually just drape his arm around their shoulders or loosely around their waists like it was nothing. Like it meant nothing. That's why it always surprised me when he held me like he did, like he was letting me know much he cared about me and couldn't get enough of me. I don't know how to explain it, but it felt like every touch meant something.

He pulled me closer until our faces were inches apart. His arms were now around my waist, holding me in place. "I forgot to tell you how sexy you looked last night." His eyes danced around my face. I didn't say anything, I couldn't. He has this strange way of leaving me speechless. "Spend the day with me?" he whispered.

In a second I would have said yes, but at that moment I realized I had work today. Why today? It was 9:30am and I had to be at Starbucks by 10:00am. I had 30 minutes to brush my teeth, shower, get dressed and walk to work. "I would love to..." He smiled big, "...but, I can't. I have to be at work in 30 minutes. I need to get ready now."

Took so much for me to pull away from his embrace, it always did. But even more so then than before because I wanted so bad to spend the day with him. We've spent the day together before but this time would be different because we wouldn't just be hanging out. No, we would be doing things together as a couple, him and I. Me and him. As an us. I loved the idea of that... us. It sounded right.

I hurried off into the shower and wrapped myself in a towel. I walked out of the bathroom and Ryan was still there, waiting by my dresser. "You're still here?"

He shifted from side to side with his hand on the back of his neck. He always did that when he was nervous. "Yeah, I- I wanted to ask you something."

"Okay... Ask away."

"Well, um. What are you doing Friday?" where was he going with this? That's a weird question to ask.

"I don't know yet. Why?"

"I was thinking. We should do something, like go out." He raised his eyebrows, anxiously waiting to hear what I had to say.

Wait. He's asking me out. I know it's weird, but I didn't expect him to ask me out. But him asking me out did strange things to me. I started to feel like that geeky 14 year old girl that just got asked out by that "popular" guy in school. I almost laughed out loud thinking about it.

I stepped closer to him, pulled the towel that wrapped around my head to let my hair down and looked up at him innocently, "Like a date?"

He chuckled and helped me dry my hair with the towel, "Mmm, like a date. Our very first date."

I pretended to think about it, "I'd love to go out with you."

"Good." He leaned down and gave me a quick kiss on the lips, "Now get dressed before I lose my self control and end up making you late for work."

I got dressed and he gave me a ride to work.

"Ugh, my head is killing me!" Kayleigh groaned. "I'm never drinking again."

My head was hurting too, but I was too happy to even complain about anything. "You know you don't mean that." I said referring to her last statement. "People only say that when they get a hangover. Don't be so dramatic."

"Doesn't your head hurt too? Last night was crazy." She had her head cradled in her hands, "But SO worth it. I finally met that guy you've been trying to set me up with."

"Logan Martinson?" I squealed. She nodded enthusiastically.

She sighed happily, "He's such a hunk."

I giggled. She had a cheesy smile on her face. "Told you so. I knew you two would hit it off."

"Yeah. But what about you huh? Did you have a good time last night?" she asked with raised eyebrows. She clearly wanted me to tell her all the juicy details.

I bit my bottom lip trying to keep my smile from getting too big, "Mm. I had a great time." This time she smiled with me and looked super excited. "And, get this, he asked me out on a date. How cute is he?"

She squealed and jumped up and down, "No way! Oh my God! Ryan never asks girls out on a date! He seriously loves you! How cute is that? Best friends falling in love! Aww! Where is he taking you? He must have something special planned. I mean, this is Ryan Monroe we're taking about. He sweeps women off their stiletto covered feet. Oh my God! We have to go shopping for the perfect first date outfit!"

Yup, that was Kayleigh. Give her a little bit of exciting news and she'll go on and on, saying things that didn't make sense, and jumping to ridiculous conclusions. I love her but sometimes it's a little too much. Especially now. We were at work and customers were staring at us.

"Kayleigh! Breathe." She inhaled slowly then exhaled. She looked calm and serious for one second but her excitement took over once again. But this time she was quiet. "First of all, I know! I don't think he's ever asked anyone out. And second, in love? Kayleigh, it's our first freaking date, we are not in love. In like, maybe. But in love? Come on. I don't even know where he's taking me. He didn't say anything. And lastly, I rarely wear stilettos."

"You know he loves you! Why else would he be trying so hard? You should text him. Ask him where you're going on your first date so you know what to wear. You don't want to be too dressed up or too dressed down."

She was right, I want our first date to be perfect and it wouldn't be cool if I showed up looking like I was ready to go to the Oscar's when we were just going bowling or something.

"Hmm... maybe you're right. I'll text him."

Ryan's POV

"Can we just play Call of Duty? I don't want to watch chick flicks!" Kenny complained

Okay, this may seem pathetic but I can't think of a better idea. I've never taken any girl out on an actual date. I've taken girls out for drinks but never out for a date with the intention of wanting to build an actual relationship. I want something more with Alison. I want to know everything about her. After 3 years of friendship, I still discover new things about her. So now I had to make our first date special. It had to be perfect because she deserved nothing less. What better way to come up with a perfect date idea than getting inspiration from chick flicks? Alison loved watching them. I've heard plenty of "Aww"s and "how cute"s come out of her pretty little mouth while watching these movies. So studying these movies was the best thing to do.

"Dude, I only have 3 days to come up with something so freaking out of this world fantastic and I'm not wasting any time playing C.O.D."

He looked at me like I was crazy. "It's the first date. Make it simple, nothing too extravagant. She'll be fine with anything"

"Yeah I know, but it's OUR first date. It's not like her and I are strangers going out trying to get to know each other. We've known each other for three years. Shouldn't it be, I don't know, more than simple?"

He shrugged as I put in How to Lose a Guy in 10 Days in the DVD player. 10 minutes into the movie, Kenny groaned for the tenth time as I tried to get into the movie. Anna walks into the living room and just stops and stares at us. "Umm. Am I interrupting something? Are you two on a date?" she teased.

"Babe..." Kenny groaned again. But he knew she was kidding. I just glared at her. She sat on Kenny's lap.

"No seriously, are you?"

"Ha. Ha. Very funny." I said sarcastically.

"Okay, well then what are you doing?"

"Getting date ideas."

"Really?" I nodded not looking at her. I was trying to focus on the movie. "You know, you and Alison are so weird. You guys worry about impressing each other and you get nervous around each other when you two are best friends. It's almost like you forget that you know each other. You don't have to worry about that stuff, just be yourself. Alison would be fine with anything as long as it's with you."

She was right. I'd be happy just spending time with her because I love being around her, because I care about her. And because she wanted to give us a chance, that meant that she wanted to spend time with me.

"So something sweet and simple?" I asked

"Duh" was all Anna said.

"That's what I told you to do!" Kenny complained.

Chapter 15

Ryan's POV

"So you're really not going to tell me what we're doing?" Alison pouted. She purposely popped out her bottom lip and made her eyes big and sad looking. I smiled at her attempt to make to tell her and shook my head. "Not even where we're going?" Her bottom lip popped out even more.

"Put that bottom lip back in your mouth. I am not going to tell you, no matter how cute and adorable you are."

"Hmm... just cute and adorable huh?" her soft delicate fingers and eyes started at my chest and gently grazed my bare skin traveling down to my stomach. She stopped just above my board shorts and slowly looked up at me. This time she bit down on her bottom lip making me bite down on my bottom lip. She was making it so hard for me to keep our date a surprise and her black bikini definitely wasn't helping.

"Cute, adorable, sexy, gorgeous. But I'm still not caving. I want to surprise you."

She put her forehead against my chest and groaned, "Fine." I laughed and hugged her around her shoulders. She suddenly looked up at me with a slight smile on her pink lips, "I hate you, you know that? You know I hate surprises."

"No, you love me. And you'll love surprises after tomorrow night, I promise." I winked at her.

She wrinkled her nose, "Love you? Hmm... maybe." She teased. Neither of us has said those three words, I love you, to each other seriously. We loved each other as friends but as boyfriend and girlfriend... not yet. I mean, I love her in a way different than I love anyone else, I know that much. I don't even know what it feels like to be in love. But we haven't even established what we were. I don't know how these things work. I don't know when it's the right time to ask her to be my girlfriend. Do I even have to ask? I had no idea how this dating relationship thing worked. I had no idea how to be a boyfriend, let alone a boyfriend that she deserved. I was completely lost when it came to being in an actual relationship. We kind of went out of order, or so I think. We've kissed and made out way before we even went out. Everything was just so new to me.

"Maybe?" I asked and she grinned and nodded, "I don't think like that answer."

"That's too bad." She said smiling, clearly aware of what I was going to do next. She stepped back and looked like she was going to make a run for it. Before she could get away I threw her tiny little body over my shoulder and ran towards the ocean. This wee little thing was like a feather, she's so small. She's petite compared to the girls I've been with. She's only 5'4 and even though the girls the other girls I've been with were as thin and slender as she was, they didn't nearly fit as perfectly in my arms like she did. Girls today are way too skinny, but her, she's perfect. Whenever I scooped her up in my arms, she fit perfectly.

I plunged into the water with her in my arms. The whole time, she was laughing, smiling, and holding onto me tightly. Most girls would freak out and complain that they we're getting their hair wet and that their make up would get ruined but she didn't care. I loved that about her. She's feminine but not too girly.

One minute she's splashing water on me and the next she was clinging onto me. Then I realized she was shivering. She had goose bumps. The water wasn't too cold for me but she was tiny compared to me. The coldness of the water affected her faster than it did me. "You're cold, let's get a towel around you."

"No, I'm fine. Just hold me." I chuckled; she's always so stubborn.

"Come on, let's get you warmed up. If you catch a cold, you won't be able to see what I've planned for our date tomorrow night."

She finally gave in and released her grip from me just enough so that we could walk back to shore. Once we got to shore, I wrapped the big beach towel around her and tried to warm her up.

Alison's POV

"Little girl, would you sit still! You're gonna have uneven eye shadow!" Anna scolded me at I tried to keep myself composed. But I couldn't I was nervous and excited. I couldn't wait to see what Ryan planned for our date. But mostly, I was excited just to spend time with Ryan.

I was dressed in a simple scoop neck floral print dress with a bow at the back and flats. Ryan didn't give me any hints as to where we were going or what we were doing so I had no idea if I was over dressed or under dressed. Anna was just as excited as I was but now she was pretty much annoyed with me. After she curled my hair, I kept fidgeting, constantly changing dresses and moving around. I wanted to look just perfect. Anna did my make up because the only thing I was capable of doing was applying eyeliner, mascara and gloss. I had no idea how to put eye shadow on. Supposedly there were special techniques, where different shades were applied to certain parts of the eyelid. It was confusing, but thank God Anna was practically born with a make up artist's talent.

"There. Perfect. You look just flawless." She looked at me and smiled.

"Really?" She nodded and stepped aside so that I was face to face with the mirror. I looked at myself. She was right. I looked flawless. A had a glowing dewy complexion. My cheeks were a light shade of pink and my eyelids were matching. My grey eyes looked brighter than ever.

Anna came behind me and wrapped her arms around my shoulders and looked at me through the mirror, "I feel like a proud mother sending her daughter off on her first date." I smiled at her genuine happiness for me. Anna was always the first to joke around and tease but it was rare when she showed her soft side. I've only seen it a few times during the course of our friendship. Once when she told me about seeing her niece being born, another when she told me that she was falling in love with Kenny, and now. "Oh come on, let's go before I get hysterical and start to ball like a little baby."

I made my way out of my room to the top of the staircase. I looked towards the bottom and saw him. A brilliant smile made it's way across his gorgeous face when he saw me. My heart missed a beat and started to beat faster and faster. My heart always did this whenever I was around him, sometimes I think I might suffer from some heart condition if it kept missing beat like it did. I thought Chris made me feel special but Ryan, he made me feel wonderful, amazing, and beautiful. It's not that Chris wasn't a great guy, it's just that Chris wasn't Ryan. Even if Chris was the most handsome, kindest, loving guy, he wouldn't be able to make me feel the way Ryan made me feel. It took only one kiss from Ryan to make me forget every single kiss from Chris. Ryan's just that guy. That guy for me.

I slowly walked down the stairs and once I got to the bottom he took one long stride towards me, gently but swiftly pulled me towards him by the waist and planted a sweet kiss just below my ear. A spot, that when kissed, literally made me weak in the knees. I practically melted in his arms at that moment. "You look lovely." He murmured ever so quietly into my ear. His warm breath across my neck made me shiver in delight.

"Thanks, you clean up nice too."

"You think so?" he asked patting down his striped button up dress shirt which made is rock hard chest and lean but muscular biceps visible through his shirt. His shirt was paired with some nice looking fitted black jeans and black converse. His attire was not so casual yet not so formal just like mine so I was definitely relieved. When I didn't say anything he added, "I do look pretty good, don't I?" He gave me a smug smile and held out his hand for me to take, "Shall we?"

I took his hand and he led to his car. He opened my door like a true gentleman and closed it when I was safely inside. We buckled ourselves in. I prepared myself for a ride that was at least 5 minutes but it only took less than a minute. I was confused. I looked out the window and saw our house. He quickly got out of the car and opened my door. He held out his hand yet again. I was even more confused, "What's going on?"

He smiled brightly, "We're here!"

"We're home?"

He nodded excitedly and chuckled, "Come on. Just follow me." He took me by the hand and led me to the side gate. As we were walking along the side of the house I tried to see where we were going but everything was black. There was absolutely no light. I instinctively clung onto his arm, "Don't be afraid, I got you."

"I'm not scared."

"Uh huh, so is that why you're cutting off the circulation in my arm? Not that I don't love it." I could tell he was smiling. I didn't answer him, I was too preoccupied with trying to find some light. Our backyard has never been this dark. Suddenly he tries to pull his arm out of my grasp but I hold on tighter. He can't leave me alone in the dark! "Wait right here." Then he was gone.

"No! Ryan, come back." I pleaded.

He chuckled and said, "Just wait a sec, will you? Trust me."

I was basically shaking in fear trying to imagine the worst possible things that would be lurking in the dark. In a few seconds I imagined, vampires, zombies, a psycho killer, even a gremlin. He wasn't seriously planning on leaving me in the dark all by myself! This better not be our date.

About 15 seconds passed, then suddenly light. Light! My eyes had to adjust to the change in brightness. And once I finally was able to see what was illuminating the dark, I lost my breath. I was amazed, mesmerized, and shocked. The gazebo that we haven't had the time to set up was built. It was standing strong and tall with twinkling lights hanging off the borders. It looked so pretty. Under the gazebo was a table with dinner for two set beautifully with a single candle light on top. And right beside the table stood Ryan with a big gorgeous grin resting on his face, "So? How'd I do?"

"Wow." Was all I managed to get out of my mouth.

He walked over to where he left me and reached his hand out to hold mine, "So I did good?" I looked up at him and nodded happily, "You're adorable, you know that?" He kissed the tip of my nose. He's said that to me a millions time before but it sounded different this time and I liked it so much that it made me blush. "Come on, let's eat before the food gets cold."

He pulled the chair out for me and I sat down. First we ate the salad, then the chicken parmesan, "Mm. This is delicious! You never cook around the house, I forgot that you can actually cook."

He chuckled with his mouth closed because he had food in his mouth and he sexily wiped his mouth with his napkin and replied, "Thanks. I would cook more if you just asked."

"Looks like I'll be asking more often, then." He smiled and held a playful gaze a little longer. "I have to tell you. I was a little surprised when you asked me out." He gave me a questioning look. "I mean, you are Ryan Monroe." I teased

He chuckled, "I may be Ryan Monroe but you're the gorgeous Alison Stewart."

"Mm, now I can see why girls can't seem to say no to you. You're such a smooth talker." I joked

He smiled and shook his head, "Very funny. You're so ridiculous, you know that?"

"If I'm so ridiculous, why did you ask me out? You have your pick of all the tall, blonde, skinny girls that fawn over you, why me?" I challenged him

"Because I like short, brunette, perfect girls like you." He replied simply. Not that I didn't like his answer but I actually wanted to know why he liked me. After 3 years of being just friends, I needed to know why he wanted me all of a sudden. "Honestly?" I nodded and he looked at me seriously, "You're different unlike every other girl I've been with. You're not annoying. You don't try too hard to be cute or sexy, you just are. You're intelligent, kind, so so sweet, and genuine. I never get tired of your teasing, or the way you call me out when I get a big head. You keep me interested, excited, and on my toes. And you're so freaking cute, how could I not ask you out?" I just smiled and he continued, "Why are you so surprised? I asked you out back in freshman year. I liked you then, and I still like you now."

"You were so not serious when you asked me out back then. I mean, you were made out with some chick the night you asked me out."

"Let me remind you, that is the same night we first met. I didn't even know who you were when I was with her."

"But how could you ask me out that same night? Can you blame me for rejecting you?"

"Honestly, I just met that girl my first night here at University. We hooked up once and that was it. It was my first week in college. I guess I got too excited. I didn't know I'd end up meeting an amazing girl like you." He said seriously.

"If you really did like me, why did you wait three years?" I asked

He paused for a moment, "Well, to be honest. I don't really deal with rejection well. You said no, so I just let it go even though we did hit it off that first night. I wasn't planning on seeing you again but then we started seeing each other more because Anna and Kenny dragged us along with them. I started liking you even more but you always seemed to make it clear that we were always going to be just friends. And when you brought Chris over, something didn't sit right with me. I didn't want you to be with him. I wanted you to be with me. I know I shouldn't have waited this long but we're now. And I'm glad you said yes this time"

I smiled, "Me too."

"And I can honestly say that the last three years with you have been the best. Even though you make fun of me most of the time, you're entertaining."

"Hmm. So what's gonna happen when you get bored with me?" I joked

His playful, sexy smile turned into a serious expression, "I don't think that'll ever happen."

The rest of dinner went by perfectly. He cleared the dishes. I offered to help but he wouldn't let me. When I thought our date was over I felt like it was the right time to say, "I had so much fun tonight."

He gave me a confused look, "Date's not over."

"It's not?"

"It's only nine o'clock. You don't seriously think the only thing I've planned was dinner?"

I shrugged, "Well, dinner was amazing. You must have spent so much time setting up the gazebo, hanging up the lights, and cooking. All of that was more than enough for me."

He laughed a little, "It's amazing how little it takes to make you happy." He smiled warmly "Even if dinner was enough for you, I still have one last thing for us to do."

"What's that?"

"A movie."

"A movie?"

"Mm. Dinner and a movie. I heard it's sort of a popular choice for first dates." He took my hand in his again, "Ready?"

I followed him and he was leading us to another dark area. "Where are we going?"

"You'll see."

We walked to the other side of the backyard. I saw our outside couch set in front of a large projection screen. There were lots of comfy pillows and a throw resting on the couch. I sat on the couch and got comfortable while he set up the projector. "So what are we watching?"

He looked at me with an amused face, "You don't like letting me surprise you, do you?" I shook my head, "Yeah, well, that doesn't surprise me." He started the movie and quickly sat right beside me and pulled me into his arms. "We're watching, The King and I." I looked at him with a questioning face. "I remember you telling me that you use to watch it with your grandpa when you were younger. And you said you loved it and never got tired of watching it."

"You remember that?" I couldn't believe it. I probably told him that once, years ago. I don't really talk much about my grandpa because it always ends with me feeling sad. Right now, he's in his critical stages of Alzheimer's disease. And now he doesn't even remember who I am. But this, doing something that reminds me of the good times I had with my grandpa is beyond amazing.

He simply nodded, "Yeah. And I bought it on DVD so you can watch it whenever you want." I just stared at him in disbelief. Who is this guy? I knew he was thoughtful... sometimes. But this. Remembering something like this really took me by surprise. He had no idea how much this meant to me. "What? Is there something on my face?"

I shook my head, "No, it's just- I mean, you keep surprising me. That's all."

"Oh, so now you love surprises, don't you?" he teased

All I could do was nod and stare at him.

He just smiled and kissed my forehead, "It's starting." He draped his arm around my shoulder and I leaned up to kiss him on the cheek.

"Thanks."

"You can thank me later with a goodnight kiss." He winked and pulled me closer as I snuggled into his body.

When the movie was over, we chatted a little bit and he walked me to my door. It's a little weird that he did that because we live in the same house but he did it anyway. While we were in front of my door we did the usual end of the first date thing.

"Well, I had an amazing time. Thank you" I said smiling up at him.

"Ditto." He replied, smiling at me too. I know right now it seems like we're being awkward with each other but we weren't. We both knew what was coming next. We were just being playful and waiting to see who would make the first move. He looked at me with raised eyebrows and tilted his head waiting for me to lean in but I didn't I stayed put.

"Okay, well goodnight." I said quietly

And before I could even touch the doorknob he stepped towards me and snaked one arm around my waist while the other gently cupped my chin. He slowly tilted his head to plant a sweet kiss on my lips. My eyes fluttered closed. His soft, warm, plump lips lightly pressed against mine. It was slow and blissful. He pulled away slightly but I felt him smiling against my lips.

"I think a second date is order." he murmured against my lips.

"Mmm. Second, third... hundredth."

I opened my eyes slightly and saw him looking at me with smiling eyes. We were still locked in our very intimate position. His smile grew wider and he gave me another short but sweet kiss. "I'd love that."

He pulled away from me and said, "Thank you for saying yes, Miss Stewart."

I nodded, "Anytime, Mr. Monroe."

"Goodnight."

With that he walked towards his room and I slipped into mine. One thought crossed my mind. Best. First. Date. Ever. I was completely blown away from beginning to end. I had a silly smile plastered across my face the rest of the night. Ryan is completely and utterly incredible. After a night like this, I know it won't be long before I'm madly, deeply, truly in love with his guy. This could probably be the start of something amazing.

17

CHAPTER 16

A lison's POV

Here we are, in an intense lip lock. My back is up against the wall and there is not on centimeter between us. Ryan's been holding onto me like he'd never let go. Don't Look Now by Far East Movement ft. Keri Hilson was playing loudly in the club. I could feel the bass bumping in my veins. I'm caught up in his embrace, feeling every caress, grab, and squeeze. With my eyes closed I savored this amazing feeling. I would've cared that anyone could see us, but at that moment I really didn't care. I loved this. I loved his lips on mine. The Keri Hilson's part was clearly playing in my head.Hey, uh, I know I promised you I'd take it slowI know I swore on everything I ownBut I can't resist, how's just one kiss?But don't look nowYou've got me going, I'm going, I'm gone.Don't look nowYou've got me going, I'm going, I'm goneDon't look nowI can't resist, how's just one kiss?Don't look now.I've never felt like this. Like I didn't have control of my body. Everything he was doing to me made me want to do the same to him. I wanted to make him feel the way I did. His lips gently traced my jaw as his hands slowly went my blouse. He didn't go further. His warm hands gently massaged the skin on my hips. My hands involuntarily went to his head. My fingers tangled in his soft dark brown hair. Then I felt him... Like really felt him on my stomach. To be honest, I was a little freaked out. I knew what that was, and I knew what he wanted."Too fast." I breathed out.He was trying to catch up with his breathing. His face remained on my neck and once he had control of his breath he pulled away slightly and faced me. I've only had my eyes closed for 20 minutes max, but I missed those beautiful hazel eyes. In his eyes I saw lust, desire, and want. He looked down at me seriously and said, "Sorry"He knew I don't do things like this. I don't publicly grope my boyfriend. It's just not me, but when I'm with him anything goes. "It's okay. You want to dance?"He smiled, "Um, actually, I'm kind of thirsty. You want anything?""Just water, please?""Okay. Be right back." He kissed me on the cheek and fought through the crowd to get to the bar.I sat back in our group's booth and waited for him to come back. I looked to the dance floor and saw Anna and Kenny in their own little world, as usual. They are so in love. And saw Kayleigh, Collin, and Kayleigh's friend Alex walking towards the booth. They had just been dancing and were sweating with smiles on their faces."Having fun?" I asked"Tons! But probably not as much fun as you." Collin teased. All I could do was blush. "So I'm guessing, things between you two are good?""Better than good. He's really everything I never expected him to be." I replied. He's been doing great for a guy that's never been in a committed relationship."So, how is he in bed?" Alex asked. Collin and I shoot her a are-you-kidding-me look. Because anyone that knew me personally knows that even if I were intimate with someone that I would never discuss the details. "What? I just want to know. We've all heard how good he is." she said simply.Collin just looked at me and Kayleigh gave me an apologetic look for her blunt friend. "We haven't done it yet." I said. I mean, there's nothing to hide. I'm not ashamed of being a virgin. I want my first time to be with someone I love. I know a lot of girls say that, but it's true.Before Alex could say anything else, Ryan came back with drinks in his hand. Thank God, he's here. He gave Kayleigh a kiss on the cheek and Alex a friendly hand shake. Once he saw Collin, he gave him 'the guy nod' and shook his hand. We've all gotten pretty close over the last few weeks. After I told Ryan Collin was gay, everything got better. They've even gone shopping once. And I have to say with the help of Collin's styling Ryan dresses even sexier now, which is something I thought was impossible."So what did I miss?" Ryan asks as he sits close to me and puts his arm around my waist."Nothing!" I say a little too quickly. Smiling sheepishly at him he gives me a questioning look and turns to Collin to get some hints. I didn't want him to know we were talking about our sex lives or rather, lack there of. I shoot Collin a don't-you-dare look. And before I can do the same to Alex she speaks."We were just talking about how good you are in bed." She says nonchalantly. Oh my goodness. Was this girl for real? I couldn't help but look away from Ryan. I knew he was looking at me. Kayleigh got up and started to drag Alex with her."I'm so sorry. We'll be right back." Kayleigh said.This was way awkward. Everyone was quiet then Collin excuses himself. CURSE HIM for leaving me!I still didn't dare to look at Ryan. I felt him shift beside me. "Alison?" he said quietly but loud enough for me to hear.I shut my eyes tightly and turned to him quickly and smiled tightly, "Can we talk about this later?" I asked even though I don't intend on bringing it up ever again. His face was serious but he nodded anyways.We went home about an hour later. While I was getting ready for bed I heard a knock on my door."Come in." I said Ryan popped his head in and had his hand over his eyes, "Are you decent?" I had to smile at that. "You're such a dork. Why would I tell you to come in if I wasn't decent?" "Umm, I don't know. Maybe to seduce me?" He winked. "Are you seduceable?" I questioned with raised eyebrows. He walked into my room, shut the door behind him and said in a very sexy voice, "Very." I shook my head and laughed. He's so ridiculous. He sat on the edge of my bed while I put lotion on my arms. He just watched me and his face turned serious, "So about earlier tonight." he started. Oh, crap. I thought we were never going to discuss this. Why did he have to remember? "You told them we were having sex?" "Huh?" I asked stupidly. "What? No! I didn't! I told them we haven't." "Then why did Alex say that you were talking about how good I am in bed?" "She was talking about it. Not me. She was telling me about what she's heard from other girls." "Oh" he said looking down. "I'm sorry. You've never had to wait before and here I am making you wait for something that every girl would give you without hesitation." He looked at me like I was crazy but I couldn't stop myself from talking, "I'm not trying to be a tease or anything like that, but I'm a virgin. You know that. And I just want it to be special. It's not that I don't think it will be special with you. I want to have sex with you, I really do." He chuckled at that. "Alison..." he said but I kept going. Everything was just coming out of my mouth, like word vomit. "But I'm not ready. You're my boyfriend and..." He stood up and shook me gently by the shoulders, "Alison!" I just looked up at him with wide eyes.

Ryan's POV

She called me her boyfriend. Her boyfriend. I had no idea that one word, 'boyfriend', could make me happy. When her perfectly pink lips said that word, I couldn't help but smile. "Breathe." I told her. She was nervous. She only rambled like that when she was nervous.

Sex is a topic that she had always been uncomfortable talking about. She's so innocent when it comes to being intimate and I don't know why but it was a turn on. She inhaled deeply and exhaled slowly. Her mouth made an 'O' shape. She's such a cute little thing. She was still looking at me with big, worried eyes. "You okay?" I asked. She just nodded. "Listen, just because we're together doesn't mean I expect us to have sex. I mean, I want to but it doesn't have to happen right away. Like I said before, I want to be with you because I actually care about you. And because I care about you, I don't want to rush into anything. When that time finally comes, it will be special because we both want it." Her face softened. "You decide when you're ready, and if it gets to be too much for you. Just tell me when to stop and I will. I'll wait until you're ready." "Here I am getting all flustered while you being your cool self are relaxed. How are you so sweet and understanding with me?" "It's easy when I have a seriously cute girlfriend like you." Being her cute self, she wrinkled her cute little nose and laughed. "You called me your girlfriend." My hands slid down her sides and stopped at her hips. "Well, aren't you?" I pulled her closer to me. She smiled at me, "Yes, I am." "Good, because I love the way it sounds." "Me too, boyfriend." She said it again. She called me her boyfriend. "Say it again." I told her. She tilted her head and smiled as she whispered, "Boyfriend." I watched as her lips moved to say it. I didn't think she could say it sexier but she did. I bent my head in to kiss her sweet lips. She moaned into my lips. Wow, even her moans are sexy. I am so turned on right now. She brought her arms around my neck and pulled me closer. I cocked my head to the side to deepen the kiss. "Would it be too much if I asked you to say with me tonight?" she whispered against my lips. "That depends." she tilted her head and smirked at me. "Will you be seducing me?"

She giggled and shook her head, "Well then, I guess we could cuddle. Unless you have other things in mind..." I wiggled my eyebrows. She laughed and playfully slapped my chest, "Hey! I thought you said you'd wait until I'm ready!" "I'm joking." I said and pulled away from her and headed straight for her bed, "Now, I'm getting in bed before you change your mind" She rolled her eyes and slipped under her covers and said, "It's not like we haven't slept together before." Now we both had our heads resting on pillows. We were facing each other. I scooted closer to her and said, "Yeah, but before we were just friends, you were untouchable. Now, we're together. I'm your boyfriend and you're my girlfriend. And as your boyfriend, I get to do things like this." I slid my hands around her waist and pulled her into my body. She smelled so good. I could smell her fruit shampoo. I loved it. She didn't protest. She settled into me and relaxed. I've never spent a night with a girl without having sex. I've only done it with her and I've never felt so content. Just holding her and feeling her heart beat close to mine felt right. This is where I want to be. Close to her.

Chapter 17

Alison's POV

Okay, so I have to admit that I'm quite awful at cooking and baking and everything else that has to do with making food. But I've been doing this every year for the past three years for Ryan's birthday. Alright so, Anna usually helps me through most of it but she's not here. She went away with Kenny, yet again. But she'll be back before lunch. And I can't not make Ryan his birthday cupcakes just because Anna isn't here. And plus, I want him to be in a good mood when I tell him I want him to be my date at my sister's wedding. He'll be meeting my wonderful family. We've been dating for about two months now and I feel like it's the right time to bring him home. I'm crazy about him and I just want my family to meet the guy that makes me happy. My family means the world to me but meeting the parents could be a little scary. I just want him to say yes.

I've just finished making the batter and placing them in little cupcake cups. I put the first batch of cupcakes in the oven and set the timer. While I wait, I check and reply to some e-mails until I hear the smoke alarm go off. Oh no, my cupcakes! I quickly head towards the kitchen and immediately turn off the oven. I start to fan the smoke away from the smoke detector in hopes of silencing the annoyingly loud beeping. But I fail. Because I'm so vertically challenged, my fanning techniques are ineffective. Then suddenly, Ryan appears out of nowhere, dressed in just his boxers with his hair disheveled. He effortlessly reaches above my head, and I can see the muscles on his body flex beautifully. Wow... he's so... sexy. I'm caught up just staring at his body but snap out of it once the smoke detector stops beeping. I look up at him and he exhales and glances down at me, "Are you okay?" he asks.

I nod as he walks over to the oven and pulls it open. Smoke escapes as he reaches in and pulls out my black, burnt, ruined, cupcakes. What went wrong? I followed the instructions. I set the timer. The timer didn't go off. Is something wrong with the timer? I looked at the timer... it was still ticking. Did I forget something? As I think through all the things that I could have forgotten, I slightly glance at Ryan and he's just smirking at me. Clearly amused. "Don't smile at me. I just ruined your birthday cupcakes!"

"How can I not smile? Here you are in your little pink apron, with your ingredients perfectly aligned, and a batch of charcoal black cupcakes." He chuckled.

It's not fair that he's half naked in this hot kitchen, looking oh so irresistible with his messy hair pointing in all directions. I can't even feel slightly insulted, I'm too distracted by his sexiness. Why does my boyfriend have to be so yummy? Focus on the cupcakes, I tell myself. I'm trying so hard to not stare at his toned abs but I can't help it. He mistakes my staring for sadness because of the cupcakes, "Hey it's okay. I'm sure they're somewhat edible." He picks one up, frowns and says, "Or not... how about I just help you make the next batch?"

"No! I'm suppose to make it for you. You can't let you make your own birthday cupcakes."

"Fine, how about I just help you figure out what went wrong?" He grabs the cookbook as I pull myself up to sit on the counter. Before I could say no he asked, "Are you really going to refuse the birthday boy on his birthday?" He looked at me with big eyes. I sighed and gave in.

He placed the cookbook on my lap and started listing off the things I was suppose to mix. I did everything correctly. Now, I'm really stumped. How the heck did those cupcakes burn? Then he suddenly says, "Oh! Here's something you definitely didn't follow."

I perk up. Finally, I'll know what happened, "What did I forget to do?"

I try to look over at what he's reading in the book but he brings it up to make it look like he's reading closely and carefully says, "It says, do not let Alison Stewart make these cupcakes. They will get burnt."

He slowly looks up at me with a gorgeous smile on his lips. He thinks he's funny. Teasing me like that. I try to act offended but the apparent smile on my face betrays me. "Ha. ha. Very funny Monroe." He chuckles and flashes an adorable smile, "Not only will you not get birthday cupcakes, you won't get the gift I spent weeks trying to get."

His jaw drops in pretend shock but it's quickly replaced with a smug smile as he shrugs, "That's okay, all I wanted was a birthday kiss from you anyways."

"You're not getting that either." I retorted. I stuck my tongue out at him and looked away to the side.

He placed the cookbook on the counter beside me and I felt his warm hands skim the bare skin on the top of my thighs. I felt my heart beat accelerate with anticipation of what he would do next. I remained still, looking to the side until he slid his hands to my hips and around my waist. He pulled me towards him so that my bottom was slightly off the edge of my counter. One leg on each side of his waist. "Come on. Don't be mad at the birthday boy." he cooed, "I was just teasing." I felt his hot breath hoover over the side of my neck.

"So was I." I breathed as I turned and looked at him.

His eyes were darker and sexier. His lips parted as he eyed mine. Slowly, he brought his lips closer to mine until they connected. His lips were gentle as I felt his grip on me tighten. He skillfully slipped the tip of his tongue into my mouth. I unknowingly ran my hands up his bare chest and slid them around his neck to bring him closer. And when he's tongue started to dance with mine my legs wrapped around his waist involuntarily.

"You taste sweet." he murmured against my lips and trailed kisses down to the base of my throat.

I giggled, "I tried the frosting."

He "mmm"ed into my neck. I felt his chest rumble against mine when he did that. His lips made its way back to mine.

Then suddenly a loud familiar voice rang all around the room, "Ohmigod. Please tell me you guys aren't fornicating in our kitchen."

Our lips parted and Ryan dramatically rested his head on my shoulder and groaned into my neck, clearly not happy that we have been interrupted. I look forward and see Anna with bags dropped on the floor beside her. She's looking at me smirking and Kenny is just being Kenny. He's calm with a slight smile on his face.

"Thanks a lot, Anna", Ryan sarcastically said into my neck.

Aww, poor guy. I just stroked his hair and smiled. He's so cute. He was still holding onto me. Kenny tugged my best friend away into her room and left Ryan and I alone. I continued to run my fingers through his hair, "They're gone" I whispered.

He lifted his head and said, "They ruined my birthday kiss." He frowned slightly and pouted.

I couldn't help but laugh, he looked genuinely disappointed. Gave him a quick peck on the lips and hopped off the counter and grabbed his hand, "Come on my silly 22 year old. It's present time."

I dragged my sexy half naked boyfriend up to my room and sat him on my bed. He wasn't sad anymore. In fact, I could've sworn I saw a cheeky grin on his face when I pushed him down to sit on my bed. I pulled his gift out from the very secret hiding place, which was my desk drawer. As I handed him the wrapped present he started, "You didn't have to get me anything." I just watched him, even though he insisted that I didn't get him anything, I just had to. I knew he would love what I got him. He started to unwrapped it, "I wasn't lying when I said all I wanted was a birthday kiss from you and-" once the wrapping paper was off he stood up, "No way! Seriously?" He looked at me excitedly. I nodded and he ran up to me and literally swept me off my feet and twirled me around.

"Boys." I muttered to myself as he was spinning with me in his arms.

He thanked me repeatedly as he set me down on my feet. "How did you even- When did you- It's not even in stores yet!"

I couldn't help but laugh in amusement. My 22 year old boyfriend is so excited and giddy over a measly video game. I just shrugged, "My brother helped work on the game so I asked him if he could give me a copy."

"This is awesome. I mean, this is Black Ops! Tons of brutal missions and new weapons." he ranted.

"You're such a nerd." I joked. He stuck his tongue at me and looked at the game again. "What's the difference between this one and all the other Call of Duty's?"

"Umm, well graphics always improve. This one's more story line based. It's set during the Cold War. Ah, I can't wait to get into this."

"But, wasn't the Cold War after World War II? I don't think there was much fighting going on during that time. I mean, there was almost a nuclear war but that's about it."

He smirked, "Now who's the nerd?" I rolled my eyes, he kissed me briefly, "It's okay. I think nerds are sexy."

"So you're happy?"

He nodded and pulled me close, "Incredibly."

"So you'll more than likely say yes to whatever I ask?" I smiled up at him.

"Uh-oh." I grinned up at him and he looked scared. "What is it?"

"So... my sister's wedding is coming up." I started and paused, "And all of my family is going to be there."

"Okay..."

"And I want you to be my date... which means you'll be meeting my whole family."

Ryan's POV

Her family. She was looking at me with bright smiling eyes, but I can't. I can't handle being around families. If I can't even handle being around my on family, how can I handle being around hers?

"I can't" I said and just like that her eyes weren't so bright. There was an awkward silence. She looked away but she didn't show any sign of sadness but I knew she was hoping I would say yes. Say something, I told myself, "I'm sorry."

She looked up at me and shook her head, "No, it's okay. It's fine, really." She tried to smile but I knew she was disappointed. I saw it in her eyes.

"I'm just not ready."

"Ry, it's okay. If you're not ready, it's really okay." She reached up her tiny right hand and touched it to my cheek lovingly and smiled, "I promise"

I brought her hand to my lips and kissed it, "Really?"

She nodded and hugged me while she looked up at me, "Now birthday boy, you need to shower and get dressed for all the awesome things I have planned for you today" Then she let go and playfully pushed me towards my room.

I turned around to face her, "I can't go shirtless for the day?" I asked with a smile.

"No." She giggled. "You know how distracting it is?"

I shook my head "How distracting is it?"

She blushed and bit down on her bottom lip to keep from smiling, "Just go."

I changed and boy did this tiny girl know how to make a guy happy. She knew how much I love to watch and play basketball. NBA season just started and I've seen every Laker game. I've been a fan even before they started winning championships again. She took me to a Laker game. A FREAKING LAKER GAME. I've been only a couple times and I know how much tickets cost especially tickets for seats just 10 rows away from the court. Even if it was just regular season, tickets are expensive. But she didn't care, she said that she was excited to buy the tickets to see how happy I'd be. She didn't watch much basketball, so she didn't know much about it. But she was so excited when we arrived at the Staples Center. She also bought me a foam finger and took a picture of the two of us with it. She's a dork sometimes... but also adorable at the same time, so she's adorkable? She was mesmerized by the thousands of dedicated fans, she was cheering during the half time show, and she even participated when it was time to yell de-fense. Once in a while, during the game, I'd get distracted by how cute she was. She was actually into the game. She was booing when the ref called a bad foul. Even standing up and clapping when a big play was made. She didn't hold back anything. By the end of the night she knew who most of the players were, and what was considered a foul. This is one of the things I love about her. She's always willing to try and experience new things. And she always seems to make the most out of every situation. She's amazing.

Later that night, I already knew there was a "surprise" party planned. I walked through the front door and "SURPRISE" everyone yelled. I looked at my pretty girlfriend behind me and she smiled big. I just had to kiss her. So I did.

A couple of guys Kenny and I use to live with when we were in the dorms were at the party. Freshman year, I did a lot of stupid shit. I skipped almost all my classes and got drunk at least 3 times a week. Yeah... stupid shit. I did all this stupid shit with these guys and Kenny. I don't regret it, it was fun. But now 2 years later I don't feel like doing that anymore. Maybe once in a while but I still won't get stupid drunk. These guys are a different story. They're still partying it up like we did freshman year. They're good guys, just immature most of the time.

Sometime during the night, I'm actually drinking with those guys. Both Kenny and I are pretty buzzed and definitely on our way to being drunk. Once I knew I had enough I went to find Alison. Even though my vision was a bit impaired I spotted her easily. I know her body so well. The tiny brunette dressed in dark skinny jeans and a frilly cream colored top at the top of the staircase talking with some other girls and Anna. I couldn't really tell and I really didn't care at the moment. I made my way upstairs and before I knew it I had my arms around her, hugging her from behind. She was startled at first but once she tilted her head to see me she smiled, "Hey you, having fun?"

I nuzzled my face into the crook of her neck, she smelled so intoxicating. I loved they way she smells, the way she feels against me, the way she makes me feel with just one touch. When I didn't respond, she turned around in my arms and asked, "How drunk are you?"

"I didn't drink that much." was all I said. My words were slurring together. I didn't realize I was that drunk. She just shook her head and smiled. I don't know why, but I picked her up and walked into my room, which was just a few steps away, shut the door, and locked it. Once we were inside, I carefully placed her on the ground. I held her close and she looked up at me. She tilted her head and gave me a questioning look. I wanted her. I leaned down to kiss her and she kissed me back with the same intensity. I walked her over to my bed with our lips still locked. We fell onto the bed and continued. But once everything got too intense she pulled away. I knew it was time to stop. I rested my forehead against hers trying to catch my breath. Then I felt dizzy, my head felt heavy. I felt so out of it. As carefully as I could I rolled off of her and just laid back and closed my eyes.

I didn't feel like throwing up but I definitely felt like I was about to pass out. "You okay, Ry?" she whispered

She swept her soft warm hand across my forehead and through my hair. I opened my eyes and saw her pretty face. She looked at me with so much care and concern. I've never had anyone look at me the way she did. Just by looking into her eyes, I knew that she genuinely cared about me. So I had to reassure her I was okay, "Yeah I'm fine, I just need to rest a bit."

"Alright. I'll go get you some water, okay?" she said.

As she was about to leave I grabbed her wrist, "No, can you just stay with me?"

She smiled warmly, "Okay. But let me just tell Anna we're done for tonight." I nodded and waited for her to come back.

I felt her climb onto the bed and settle next to me. She kissed my forehead and said, "Happy Birthday, babe."

"Thanks for today."

"Don't worry about it. You had fun, right?"

I nodded, "The best birthday ever."

She smiled, "Good."

She rested her head on my chest and hugged me around my middle. For the first time in a long time, I felt like I was home. I had no idea how amazing this felt. Knowing that I had someone who sincerely cared about me. I almost forgot what it was like being care for. This girl, the girl I get to hold, kiss, and care for is making me feel of all of it. If she's this incredible, her family should be just about the same way, right? She had to come from an amazing family for her to be the beautiful person she is.

"Alison" I whispered.

"Mm?"

"Can I still be your date to your sister's wedding?"

She sat up and looked at me carefully, studying my face, "Really?"

I used all the strength left in me to sit up and nodded, "Really. If your family is half as amazing as you are, then I should be fine."

She lunged into me giving me a tight hug while tackling me onto my back, "Oh Ryan, you have no idea how much this means to me. They're amazing, I promise."

She pulled away and looked down at me. I swept the strands of hair covering her face behind her ear and said, "I'm sure they are. I can't wait to meet them"

CHAPTER 18

Alison's POV

I was ready for work, morning shift at Starbucks. I was so noisy this morning, accidentally bumping into my dresser, almost tipping over my floor lamp, and dropping my keys. I probably wouldn't have been so clumsy if I wasn't trying extra hard not to wake Ryan up. He looks so adorable when he sleeps, I wouldn't want to ruin that. He's on his stomach and the covers are slightly below his waist revealing an adorable pair of baby blue boxers. I can see the contours of his muscles as his body rises and falls slowly as he breathes. I feel a smile on my lips, my boyfriend is so sexy.

"Ry." I whispered and gently nudged him, "I'm leaving."

He stirred a bit and turned over. He opened his eyes slowly, "I'm leaving for work." I kiss him briefly on the lips. He pulls me onto him, making me lay on top of him. I couldn't help but squeal, "Ryan!"

"No" he groaned. He had his eyes closed again while he held me tight around the waist. He wouldn't let me go.

"Ryan, I have to go." I said with a laugh.

He shook his head, "Nah uh." I looked at his handsome face and traced my index finger over the bridge of his nose, then along his lips. He pretended to bite my finger but I pulled it away before he could. His eyes lazily opened up and he suddenly rolled us both over so that he was on top of me, "Let's stay in today."

He was propped up on his elbows and he was inches away from my lips. "I can't just not go to work."

He smiled seductively and bent his head to kiss my neck, "Why not?" he murmured against my skin. "We can spend the whole day snuggled up in bed." I felt my eyelids grow heavy, and before I knew it my eyes were closed. All I could think about was what he was doing to me, how amazing he was making me feel.

As usual, I took his gorgeous hair in my hands. Twirling, gently pulling and running my fingers through his luscious locks. He started to nibble and lick on the skin of my collarbone. I felt myself melting into him, arching my back. We've been in this position many times before but each time feels different, more intense, more sensual, more passionate. It just kept getting better and better. Like toe curling, back arching, mind blowing better.

"Anna will be left alone with all those customers if I don't go in" I said sounding breathless.

Then I felt his lips capture mine, "But how could you turn this down?" he said as I felt him smile against my lips.

I laughed, "Did you really just say that?" He gave me a smug smile and nodded, "You're lucky you're hot Mr. Monroe or else I'd totally be turned off by that big ego of yours." I joked.

"Oh, you think I'm hot?" he teased. I pressed my lips together while holding back a smile. "You do, don't you?" he pressed. I shook my head. "No?" he asked. And I just looked at him. Then his fingers started to tickle my sides. I immediately bursted out in giggles while squirming beneath him.

"Ryan, stop. You know I'm ticklish!" I managed to say in between laughing.

"First, you have to admit it."

"Admit what?"

"That you think I'm hot."

I didn't want to, even if it was the truth. But I had to, or else I'd pee in my pants from laughing too much, "Okay! Fine!" I said. He raised his eyebrows and waited for me to say it, "You're hot."

He smiled big, "So are you." he said without hesitation and kissed me quickly. Then he added, "That's makes us a perfect match, ey?"

I rolled my eyes with a smile and sneaked away from under him and stood up. He sat at the edge of my bed and slouched while rubbing the sleep from his eyes. I gathered my things in my arms and heard him fixing my bed behind me. Me, being the neat freak I am was appalled the first time he left my bed unmade and after that I taught him how to make a bed. Apparently, this boy has never had to make his bed, he was so use to just getting up in the morning leaving the blankets all messed up and returning at night to the same messed up sheets. I look behind me and my bed was perfectly made, I smiled proudly and made my way to him to say goodbye again.

"Now I really have to go" I tip toed and lightly kissed his lips.

He pouted, "What time will you be home tonight? We haven't had time alone in three weeks."

He's right, since school started we've both been busy. I had a job, classes, and I start volunteering at a nearby elementary school today. And he had his job, internship, and classes. We barely had time for each other anymore. The only time we could actually be alone was when we were turning in for bed.

"Well, I start at the school today. I'll be home by 7 at the latest. What about you?"

"I get off work at 7:30. Let's have dinner at Vincencio's?" he asked

"I'd love that."

He smiled that cute boyish smile, "Great. It's a date." He kissed me, this time slowly. His lips moved sensually against mine. He sucked on my bottom lip. Oh, what is he doing? I have to get to work, but he's making me want to just stay here and do this. When his tongue expertly traced my bottom lip, I moaned into his mouth.

"I'm going to be late." I whispered

"Well then, you better get going." he said, but he kissed me again. His lips would not leave mine. He knew exactly what he was doing. I didn't even notice but he was slowly walking us back to my bed, but when I felt myself fall backwards I knew I had to stop or else I'd never leave this room.

"Oh no." I said as I reluctantly withdrew my lips from his.

"What?" he asked innocently. "I was just kissing you." he said with a playful smile.

I shook my head, "Is that all?" he nodded, "Well, I REALLY have to go now."

"Okay, but just one more kiss." I narrowed my eyes at him and he pouted and held up his index finger for just one.

"Just one, then I'm out of here." I kissed him quickly and got up.

He laughed, "That was not a kiss."

He came forward to kiss me but I put my hand to his mouth, "Well, I guess you'll just have to wait until tonight, then."

I removed my hand from his lips. "Fine." he said with a smile, "I'll see you tonight."

Ryan's POV

I'm at Vincencio's waiting for my girlfriend, she already told me she'd be late. We're going to have sometime to ourselves, time that we haven't had in weeks. Over the summer we spent everyday together and now that school has started we've been too busy with volunteer work and internships. We had no free time. All our free time was spent sleeping or studying. Tonight would be just us, nothing to worry or think about.

I feel two arms wrap around my neck from behind. I tilt my head to see her, she smiles and kisses me tenderly, "Hey, I'm so so sorry I'm late."

"It's alright. You hungry?" before I get up to pull her seat out she motions for me to sit back down.

She sits, "Starving!"

We order some food and while we wait we chat a little bit about our day.

"So how was the first day at the school?" I asked.

Her eyes lit up in a way I've never seen before, "Oh Ryan, it was wonderful! The teacher I work under is so amazing with the kids, which is unbelievable considering she's about 8 months pregnant. And the children are so adorable. I can't wait to go back."

It was nice seeing her excited about what she wanted to do with her life. Alison had this maternal quality about her. She would no doubt be a great mother and teacher.

"How was interning? Did they tell you if there were any job openings?" she asked

"Well, actually-" I was cut off by her phone.

She searched through her purse, "I'm sorry, I thought I turned it off." Once she found it she turned it off.

"Who was it?"

"Just Chris." she said nonchalantly. She set her purse on the back of the seat and looked at me. I was looking at her trying not to look bothered but I couldn't help it and she noticed, "What's wrong?"

"You still talk to Chris?" I asked

"Not really, we've only started talking because we're in the same group for a class presentation. That's why I was late tonight, I had to meet up with my group."

"So you were late because you were with Chris?"

"Yeah... wait no, I was with the whole group, not just Chris."

I'm not angry. I don't know how I feel. I've never had this feeling, where I was worried that the girl I was with could be taken away at any moment. I didn't know where this conversation was going, I had nothing to say.

"That doesn't bother you right? That I'm around Chris?" she asked.

"No." I shook my head. "Of course not."

Two weeks have passed and we spend even less time together.

Today I actually got out of class early so I'm going to visit my girlfriend at work. As I enter the coffee shop I can't help but notice how busy it is. The line seems never ending. I look towards the back and Alison shaking some drink in her hands while smiling. Even at work, when tons of customers are swarming around she's still smiling. Then I see who she's smiling at. Chris. She's smiling at him and he's smiling back while leaning towards her over the pick up counter. Is it bad that I'm annoyed right now?

I make my way to her and at the same time Chris is leaving. He doesn't notice me but I sure noticed him. I wasn't trying to glare or scowl, I just didn't like that he was talking to my girlfriend.

"Hey babe! What are you doing here?"

"Why was Chris here?" I ask trying as nonchalant as possible.

She looked around the surroundings like it was obvious, "Um. To get coffee?" She laughed. But her smile quickly faded when she noticed that I was uncomfortable with the situation. I could tell she didn't want to have another awkward conversation. I didn't want to have it either, but why did Chris have to come and see my girlfriend. It just bothered me. She finished making the drink and poured it into the plastic cup and placed a lid on top. She called the order out and just looked at me.

I forced myself to not continue on with the jealous boyfriend interrogation, "So how's work?"

She smiled at my lame attempt to change the subject and blew a piece of her hair away from her face, "busy." She held a playfully gaze a little longer and added, "Is that all you came here to ask me?"

"That and I wanted to see if we were still on for tonight."

"Of course"

"Alright, I'll see you at 8."

She smiled, "Okay, can't wait." And she blew me a kiss.

Alison's POV

It's 6:00 and I still have two hours before I meet Ryan at the house for dinner. I went to the library to meet up with my presentation group. We finished early and a few of the members decided we should celebrate. We've worked extremely hard on every single detail of this project and what better way to celebrate than with celebratory drinks? We went to a nearby pub and within an hour most of the group had left. Chris, Ivy, Chase and I were the only ones left. It was already 7:30 so I thought it was time for me to go home. Chase drove all of us home. I came home to a sleeping Ryan on the couch.

I gently shook his shoulder, "Hey honey."

His eyes flutter open and he smiles lazily, "Hey, where have you been?"

I check my watch, "I'm not late am I?"

"No, but I thought you got off work at 5:30?" he said as he yawned and sat up.

I sat on the coffee table so that we were facing each other, "I did but I met with my group to finish the presentation. Then we went to get some drinks."

He narrowed his eyes, "You drank with Chris?"

"Not just him, the group."

He looked irritated, "I texted and called you. Didn't you check your phone?"

"Oh no... I'm sorry, I didn't check."

"Well, I left work early to see you."

"You did?" He just looked at me, still irritated but also angry, "I'm sorry."

"Whatever" he said under his breath as he walked away from me.

Oh no, he has no right to be angry at me when I've done nothing wrong. I stood up and walked towards him, "What's your problem?" I asked

He turned around, "Nothing, I've just been waiting here to see you for 2 hours that's all" he said bitterly.

We were about a foot away from each other. He was looking down at me and I was looking up at him. "Wait a minute. I told you I didn't check my phone. I apologized and I'm here when I said I would be , why are you so mad?"

"Because instead of spending time with me, your boyfriend, you're out with your ex." as he said this I saw a hint of sadness in his eyes but he's still in the wrong here. He's angry at me for nothing.

I sighed, "I wasn't with him because I wanted to be. I was with him for the project."

I was trying to end this argument but he just kept going. "And celebration drinks were part of the project?"

"No"

"Then you weren't with him because you had to be."

"Okay, so what? We went out for drinks." I said and continued, "with the group" I stressed. "What is so bad about that?"

"What isn't bad about that? You're with him when you should be with me. I don't like it when you spend time with him."

"Why? It's not like we're doing anything. I'm not doing anything wrong." He just looked at me. "Don't you trust me?"

"No, I don't" he blurted out.

I couldn't believe it. After knowing each other for 3 years, he still didn't trust me. And he's suppose to be my best friend. I haven't done anything for him to not trust me. There was so much I wanted to say. I wanted to tell him that between the two of us, he's the one that couldn't be trusted, with his history. But I didn't want to hurt him. I didn't want to say it because despite the way he treated all those other girls, I do trust him. So I just walked away.

"Where are you going?" he asked as I walked up the stairs to get to my room.

"Leaving before I say something I don't mean."

20

Chapter 19

Alison's POV

It hasn't been five minutes since I walked away from him and he's knocking on my door. Most girls would love their boyfriends chasing after them right after a fight but me, I'm glad he's come after me, but I need a little time to think. We've never fought before and I don't know what happens next. The Ryan I'm use to is really calm, laid back and confident. But tonight he was agitated, angry and insecure. He's never been angry with me. And I've never been angry with him either. I need time to cool off, I don't want this fight to continue.

"Alison, can you talk to me please?" I hear my boyfriend say from the outside of my door.

I stare at the door for the longest time before saying, "Ry, I just need a minute."

I hear him sigh. Then within seconds I hear a thump, "Shit" I heard him groan.

I rush to the door and swing it open thinking he's hurt himself, but he's okay. "You still care about me." he says with a small smile. I can't believe he's trying to make this a joke. Is he kidding? How can he not see how serious this is? I'm getting even more angry by the minute. I narrow my eyes at him and turn away from him to return to my room but not before I feel his hand gently pull on mine, "Hey" I stop because I hear the softness in his voice, "I'm sorry."

I turn to face him and he's slightly biting on his bottom lip like he's unsure of what to say. "I'm sorry." he says again with the same gentleness I heard moments earlier. "I don't know how to do this." He started rubbing the back of his neck, "I'm sorry for the way spoke to you. I shouldn't have reacted that way."

"What was that?" He looked down, "I've never seen you that mad. And you were mad at me for nothing."

He slowly looked at me and said, "I wasn't mad at you"

"It seemed like it."

He opened his mouth to speak but stopped himself and began again, "I wasn't mad at you. I just-"

"You what?"

"I was jealous. I didn't expect to react that way." he said quietly. "I've been pretty good about it the past couple of weeks but tonight, I guess I was just angry that you spent your time with him instead of me."

"You know if I knew you came home early I'd be here with you."

He nodded, "I've just been really missing you lately. This summer, we spent nearly every second of everyday together and now that school has started, I barely see you. I miss spending time with you, that's all."

I could really see how genuine he was being. But missing me shouldn't be an excuse for him acting jealous and getting angry with me. "I know, I miss you too" I told him, "But you can't act that way just because you miss me."

He looked at me and nodded, "I know."

We stared at each other for bit, finally ending this fight. He pulled me into his arms, hugging me. I wrapped my arms around his middle with my head against his chest.

"Does this mean you accept my apology?" he whispered into my hair.

I nodded and felt him hug me tighter. I closed my eyes thankful that we were okay again. Being angry with him was the worst feeling in the world. I never knew that being angry with him would hurt me.

Still in a tight embrace I had to ask, "Did you mean it? When you said you don't trust me?"

"No. I do trust you. I know you wouldn't cheat on me. I know you would never do anything to hurt me or anyone else for that matter."

I looked up at him, "Then why did you say it?"

"It just slipped, I was angry, I didn't mean it." he said. But he saw that I was unconvinced, "I trust you." he reassured me.

At moment passed before I said, "That was our very first fight. Ever, Ryan."

"I know." He sighed.

"I didn't like it at all." I shook my head trying to forget about how horrible it was. Fighting with him was torture.

"I hated it." he admitted.

"I hate being mad at you."

"I'm sorry."

Somehow I managed to fall into a deep slumber in Ryan's arms. I was so exhausted from our fight I went straight to sleep without eating the dinner Ryan and I were suppose to have when we had a fight.

"Lovebirds" I heard Anna chirp outside my door. She knocked.

I opened my eyes and tilted my head up and saw Ryan still sleeping. We were still in our clothes from last night. I look at the clock on my night stand and it's already 11:30 am. We've slept for more than half a day. I guess last night's fight took a lot out of us. I slowly brought myself up into a sitting position with my arms. "Come in" I yawned.

Anna peaked her head in at the same time Ryan wakes up. "Hey, I was just wondering if you guys want to come us with to the beach today? It's probably one of the last time's the we'll be able to go to a warm and sunny beach for a while. It's suppose to get colder this week."

"You want to?" Ryan asks me.

"Yeah, sure. We're in." I say

"Great. We're leaving in half an hour if you want to come with me and Kenny."

"That'll be great, thanks Ann."

"Yup." she said and added, "And Ryan, no speedos, okay?"

He glared at her and sarcastically said, "Ha ha."

I slowly get off my bed and walk towards my dresser to get my bikini and a loose white top and daisy dukes, "We should probably get ready."

As I pull my bikini out of my drawer, I feel Ryan's arms snake around my waist from behind, "Maybe I should wear speedos just to mess with Anna, what do you think?" I gave him a weak laugh. I don't know why, but I'm still feeling a little bit iffy about last night. He knew something wasn't right, "You alright, babe?"

I turned and looked up at him, "Mhm. Yeah, I'm just a little tired. That's all." His face was serious, "You should get ready. I'm going to brush my teeth now." I walked to the bathroom and shut the door behind me. Come on, Alison, everything is fine now. You made up last night, stop making it a bigger deal than it has to be, I thought to myself as I looked at myself in the mirror.

I got ready and made my way downstairs. Kenny and Anna were excited as usual. They've always been that couple that loves surfing, laying out in the sun, and body boarding. They're love for the ocean has always been something that they can talk about for hours. They happily walked out the door, I followed after them but Ryan stopped me before I was out the door, "Hey, we're okay right?" he asked as he studied my face seriously.

His eyes were pleading and sad, "Yeah, of course" I smiled. We were okay but I wasn't. That little argument we had was still weighing on my heart.

He smiled a little because he knew that I wasn't telling the truth entirely but I didn't want to talk about it. I tip toed and brought his face closer to mine and kissed him, "Let's have fun today." I said.

We arrived at the beach and it was a perfectly sunny day. Perfect for laying out in the sun, barbecuing burgers and hot dogs, and surfing. As the boys played football, us girls laid out to get some color on our skin. When Anna and I were alone and while reading through magazines she asks me, "How are things with you Ryan?"

I looked at her and saw that she knew things were a bit off with me today, "We had our first fight last night." She waited for me to vent, "He got jealous that I was still talking to Chris. But the thing is, I wasn't talking to him because I wanted to but because we were placed in the same group for a presentation. And I told him that but he got angry and said that he doesn't trust me."

"Really?" She asked stunned "Ryan doesn't really strike me as the jealous type"

"I know, I'm just as surprised as you."

"Well that just shows that he cares about you a lot."

"I know, but he shouldn't be worried, there's nothing to be jealous about."

"Yeah, but guys tend to get that way sometimes. Kenny use to get jealous. It was so infuriating sometimes. We fought a lot because of it but we got through it. If we got through it so will you."

"How did you get through it?"

She tried to think back, "Hm, I'm not so sure. I think it was when he finally realized that I really actually cared about him. I had to beat it through his thick skull that I'm crazy about him and that he's stuck with me. Sometimes, they just need reassurance that you care about them as much, if not more than, they care about you." I raised my eyebrows, "I know, weird. I didn't think guys could be so insecure." She reached out and grabbed my hand in hers, "Don't worry, you'll get through it. I'm sure of it. You two are almost as perfect for each other as Kenny and me." She winked.

Anna's encouraging and supportive words lifted my spirits. It gave me hope. It was time to eat a late lunch and everyone is scattered around sitting on their beach towels. Ryan brings me a burger with potato chips on the side. He hands the plate over to me and sits beside me and says, "You must be hungry. You didn't eat dinner last night."

"A little hungry, but this will help" I smiled, "thanks."

"You're welcome. I put extra tomatoes in it and a little bit of lettuce. Just how you like it." He smiled proudly for knowing what I liked.

"Aw thanks, you know me so well, Rybear" I teased him as I pinched his cheek.

He chuckled and said, "Shh, not in public. The guys will tease me to no end if they hear you call me that."

"Ry-" I said a little louder but he held his index finger over my lips before I got the bear out.

He raised his eyebrows, "You want to be tickled?" I shook my head "I wasn't going to say Rybear."

"Uh huh." he said while looking at me sideways with a smirk, "Sure you weren't."

Even though he was acting like a jealous idiot last night, I can't ignore the fact that he's still my best friend, he's guy that can make me smile at the drop of a hat. The guy that knows me better than I know myself sometimes. And when we're together, talking and being like we are right now I can't help but realize that we are pretty perfect for each other. We're ourselves, he accepts me for who I am. And maybe he was jealous because he cares a lot about me, like Anna said.

I looked at the profile of his face and smiled because I was so lucky to have this handsome man all to myself. I kissed him on the cheek. He turned to look at me and smirked, "What was that for?"

I shrugged, "Just because."

He smiled big and kissed me on the lips slowly and tenderly, giving me our first proper kiss of the day. He pulled away slightly and tucked a piece of my hair behind my ear. I opened my eyes and smiled, "And what was that for?"

He smiled and said simply, "For being you."

Then our moment was completely ruined by Logan, Kayleigh's new boyfriend. He pretended to gag with his finger in his mouth, "Looks like Kenny and Anna have competition for being the couple most likely to make us barf all over our food." Kayleigh playfully nudged Logan in his side.

I rolled my eyes and looked at Ryan, "I think we'd win." he said.

"Whatever newbies." Anna called out smiling.

Ryan's POV

It was dark already and Alison and I were snuggled up on a blanket near the bonfire. She sat in between my legs while I had my arms around her. Katy Perry's Teenage Dream was playing softly in the background. At first Alison was just humming then it turned into singing. Her singing isn't horrible just a little off tune.

"You're cute." I said and heard her laugh a little, "but your singing ... not so much."

She turned around with a shocked look on her face. I couldn't help but laugh. She sat on her knees. And with her hands on her hips she challenged me, "Can you do any better?"

I held my index finger up and waited to jump in. I sat on my knees as she sank down to the blanket sitting on her bottom. My part was coming up and then I started to sing, "We drove to Cali and got drunk on the beach" I held up a beer bottle and wiggled it between my thumb and index finge. She smiled, "Got a motel and built a fort out of sheets. I finally found you" I pointed at her and she giggled, "my missing puzzle piece. I'm complete. Let's go all the way tonight" I moved closer to her as she reclined onto her back until I was hovering over her. She raised her eyebrows with a smirk on her pretty face, "No regrets, just love. We can dance until we die. You and I, we'll be young forever"

She watched my lips move as I sang. She ran her hands up my chest and around to the back of my neck. She brought her head up and brushed her lips against mine once I finished singing. She pulled away and set her head back down on the blanket with her hair fanned out. The light reflected off her flawless face and I saw nothing but beauty and innocence. I feel terrible for acting the way I did with her last night. How could I do that when I know she doesn't have a bad bone in her body. She chose me, not Chris. She chose me. Alison wouldn't do anything to hurt me. I can trust her.

I knew I'd care about her more than anyone else but I didn't expect to feel this way. I had no idea how intense caring about someone could be. Like my heart is being filled to capacity, and just by seeing her smile it feels like its about to burst. Caring about her does strange things to me. She makes me happy to no end. Caring more and more about her makes me even more afraid of losing her. And when I saw her and Chris together something inside me wanted to do anything and everything to keep him from stealing her away from me. I want her all to myself.

CHAPTER 20

Ryan's POV

    I'm waiting outside my car leaning against the door for my girlfriend in Fraiser Elementary School's parking lot. We're suppose to meet Kenny, Anna, Kayleigh and Logan at the costume shop to get some costumes for tomorrow night's Halloween party. Held at our house, of course. We're a little late getting costumes but the girls wanted to shop all together and this was the only time we'd all be able to meet up. I have no idea why they had to shop in a group but I guess it's important.

    I see Alison outside one of the classrooms standing in front of a line of six year olds. She puts her pointer finger on her lips and the kids all copy her. Then she puts both arms at her sides and the kids follow her movement yet again. She leads them to the tables outside and dismisses them.

    It's lunch time and all the little kids are scattered everywhere with their lunch boxes, some eating some playing with their food. This one boy was throwing pieces of bread at a girl's head. Why little boys do that? I have no clue. I threw food when I was young but never at a girl's head. Right when I was about to tell that boy it was mean to throw food at the little girl, the little girl throws little fruit snacks at his face. I chuckled, that little girl is so confident, and brave. Props to her. Then I see Alison bouncing towards me. She tiptoes and brings my face closer to hers to kiss me, "Hey" she coos. "Well hello to you too." I say, "you do know there are little children who can see what we're doing" Before she could get a word in, we hear a small child's voice, "Ew, they're kissing!" Alison sucks in her bottom lip and immediately blushes beautifully as she looks up at me. She turns around and we both see the little boy and the little girl who were having a food fight earlier. They had disgusted looks on their faces. I couldn't help but laugh. They have no idea that they'll be doing the same thing when they find that special someone. Alison bends down so that she's eye level with the little ones, "Thomas, Ginger, we were just-" The little girl named Ginger finishes Alison's sentence, "Kissing." Then they both yell, "EW!" Alison looks up at me for help but I just chuckle. These kids are too amusing. Thomas decides to ask, "Is he your booooyfriend?" Yes, he extended the word boyfriend in the same disgusted tone. "Um-" Alison starts "Yeah, am I your booooyfriend?" I tease her. She glares at me and says, "Yes. Yes he is." Ginger and Thomas look at each other with wide eyes and shout, "EW!" Oh my god, children are hilarious. Or maybe Alison being completely embarrassed is hilarious, either way, I'm laughing. "Hey, hey, what's going on here? Why aren't you eating your lunch?" a man who looks about a few years older than Alison and I asks the kids. Thomas points at us and says, "They were kissing. Isn't that gross?!" The man laughs, "Thomas, one day when you're older you're going to want to kiss pretty girls too." He then looks at Alison and winks. Did he really wink at my girlfriend? "Yeah right," Thomas says as he crosses his arms over his chest. "Yes. I'm right. Now go finish your lunch so you can play." the man says to both children. Both children run off and the man looks at me and Alison, "Kids"I laughed to be polite. And Alison spoke, "Corey, this is my boyfriend, Ryan.""Ahh, the boyfriend. We've heard so much about you. It's nice to meet you." He extended his hand and I shook it reluctantly.He was about to say something before a couple kids started screaming and yelling, he looked over his shoulder only to find some boys fighting. He sighed and said, "Well, I've got to go. I'll see you."On the drive to the costume shop, I asked Alison who he was and she said that he was the new teacher they've hired to take over for Mrs. Portman who was recently submitted to bedrest until she gives birth. I couldn't ask more about Corey because we were already at the shop. But from what Alison told me he's really good with the kids. They listen to him more than they listened to Mrs. Portman. And has almost all the kids in the class reading chapter books. She admired him and how he was able to teach the children in an effective and positive way. To someone else, they'd think that Alison was gushing over Corey but its just the way she is. She just simply admires his ability with the children, nothing more. We've already fought because I was being jealous, I don't want that to happen again. Whatever I'm feeling towards this Corey guy, I can't let it get the best of me. I can't assume the worst. I have to let it go and just remind myself that Alison's with me.

Alison's POV

The Halloween Party is in full swing downstairs. Anna and I just finished getting ready because we were busy setting up until the first guests arrived. Anna is dressed as a sexy pirate. And I'm dressed up as Tinkerbell even though I'm brunette. Everyone insisted that I dress as a fairy because of my size. We made our way downstairs, walking through the crowd of people to find our boyfriends. I was suddenly pulled into strong very familiar arms. It was Ryan. I turned in his arms and quickly kissed him. "Aww you make such a cute Peter Pan"

He chuckled, "I hope so. These tights feel strange. My manhood is suffocating and my leg hairs feel weird."

I wrinkled my nose and said, "Wouldit make you feel better ifI said you looksexy too?"

"Only if you're being honest." He smiled down at me and said, "You make such sexy tinkerbell."

"But Tinkerbell's blonde."

"Mm, true. But you're proof that Tinkerbell would look much better as a brunette." he flirted

I smiled as he bent his head to kiss me again. I felt his hands wander to my bottom. "Someone's skirt is quite short." he cooed. I felt him smile against my lips. I knew he enjoyed what he was feeling.

"Mm, I thought you'd like it."

"Oh, I like it." He kissed me again, "So, so much"

We were surrounded by people on all sides so I knew no one would be able to see us feeling each other up. Not that I cared at that moment.

We drank and danced, and drank and danced. The whole night, Ryan and I exchanged countless glances when we were talking with our friends. It was like a secret shared between the two of us and no one else. When we were both clearly intoxicated, we somehow wandered upstairs. I pulled him into my room and locked the door, both of us giggling at nothing in particular. He pressed me up against my door and immediately captured my lips with his. His knee was between my two legs. I felt myself melting and he held me up. He picked me up with my legs around his waist and walked us to my bed. Somehow, he gently places me on my bed and picks me up around the waist and slides me up so that my head is resting on my pillow. All the while, our lips are still attached. Eventually, both of us end up in our underwear. Each article of clothing was carelessly tossed aside. As he gently sprinkles tiny little butterfly kisses along my neck down to just above my breasts, he reaches behind me and swiftly unhooks my bra. Slowly, he slips my bra off and throws it to where the rest of our clothes are. I felt his hot breath hovering above my chest. Then suddenly his warm mouth was around my already pert bud. He sucked, licked, and kissed me everywhere. My body was shivering in delight. But when his hands wandered to elastic of my panties, something made me aware of what was going on. I wasn't ready.

"Ryan?" I said.

"Yeah?" he said in between kisses.

"I think it's time to stop."

He hovered above me for a couple seconds. His breathing was uneven and heavy. He kissed me one last couple of times and rolled to the other side of the bed laying flat on his back. He exhaled deeply. I hate that I always get him going and stop before it can go anywhere.

"I'm such a tease." I muttered to myself.

He turned to me and chuckled, "What?"

I try to cover myself with my comforter as I sit up. "I keep doing this to you. I get you all hot and bothered and then I stop everything before it goes any further. I'm a tease and I hate it." He laughs at me like I've said something completely insane, "Stop laughing at me. It's not funny."

"I'm sorry, but you're being ridiculous. You're not a tease, you don't do it intentionally. I mean, I get turned on by you so easily, it's not even funny. It's not you're fault that I find you sexy."

"Yeah, but you've never had to wait this long. And --" then I he kissed me. It was slow and chaste.

As he pulled away he stroked my cheek with his thumb, "You need stop worrying about this. I already told you. I'm okay with waiting. You're worth the wait."

"But what that?" I point at his erection, "Isn't that a problem?"

He chuckled, "I'm not going to die of an unreleased erection."

I looked at my very sexy shirtless boyfriend. He's my best friend, he makes me happy, he's always sweet and understanding. I know I can't picture being with any other guy but him. If I was going to have sex with any one it would be him. "Why can't I just do it? I want to have sex with you."

He chuckled and brushed a piece of my hair behind my ear. "Baby, we won't be having sex. We'll be making love. And that'll be a first for that both of us." His hazel eyes were piercing through my grey ones. He was looking at me like I was his world, "And until then, we can keep doing this."

His soft lips traced mine in a sensual way. I sighed, "How can kissing be enough when you've done much more with other girls?"

He did have to answer, I wasn't expecting him to. His past has nothing to do with us now. But he just looked at me with a cute smile on his face, "Because, when I kiss you, I actually feel something. Every kiss, hug, or glance I share with you is greater than everything I've had with those other girls. You make me feel things I've never felt before."

I lean into him so that our lips are inches apart, "Good things I hope."

He gave me a big toothy grin and said against my lips, "Mm, very good things."

He kissed me softly and we got ready for bed. When we settled under my covers he wrapped his strong arms around my waist and pulled me into him. After a few moments of silence he said, "You were really great with those kids earlier today."

I smiled, "Thanks. They're wonderful."

"Is that why you want to be a teacher? Because you like kids?"

"Mm, not only that. You remember my godson? The one I told you about?" I felt him nod behind me "Um, well when he was 5 he had trouble reading and writing. His teacher would call him hurtful names and tell his mom that he needed to be held back. I tried helping him sound out words and spell and he did just fine. It turned out it was the way his teacher was teaching was the problem. A couple of other parents complained about the teacher and she ended up getting fired. After all that, I knew that I wanted to be a teacher because I just want children to be able to learn and be themselves without being criticized and insulted. No child deserves to be unhappy. I just want every kid to be happy and know that they can do and be anything they want to be. Every kid deserves to have a happy childhood like I did."

"You're amazing." he whispered into my hair. "What was your childhood like?"

"Well, I had my brother and sister. I'm the youngest, so I'm the baby of the family. We're all really close in age so when we were really young we had our own adventures together. Sometimes, my brother would even let my sister and I play guns with him and his friends."

He chuckled and I felt his chest rumble against my back, "Bet all the little boys let you shoot them."

"No, actually they didn't care. They shot my sister and I first! So my sister and I had to find something else to do while they continued to play." He laughed a little, "What was yours like?"

I felt him stiffen behind me. "It was okay, I guess."

"What do you mean?"

"Nothing special. I had my sister and that was it."

"Oh come on. No stories about you annoying your sister?"

"Nope. Can we just go to sleep? I'm really tired."

"Is something wrong?"

"No, I'm just tired. Okay?"

"Okay"

I couldn't help but think he was hiding something. I didn't want to push it any further because I didn't want to fight. When Ryan decides that he doesn't want to talk, there's no discussion, he won't talk. Now that I think about it, Ryan has never told me about his family. Alll know is that his mom died when he was 13 and that he has a sister. I guess I never really asked again because he made it clear that he didn't want to talk about it. But now that we're together, I can't help but feel worried.

22

Chapter 21

Ryan's POV

I walk into the kitchen and see Anna, Kenny, and Alison emptying our kitchen of canned goods and nonperishable foods. I walk behind my girlfriend, hold her by the hips and kiss her on the neck just below her ear, which happens to be one of her weak spots. "Hey" I murmur against her skin. She turns around gives me the kiss on the lips I've been waiting for all day at work.

"Hey, how was work?" she asks as she puts some cans in a box.

"Good. What's going on here?" I ask

"We're donating some food to the Thanksgving food drive, remember?" Anna says as she too fills a box with food.

It must have slipped my mind. Thanksgiving is in a few days and my sister has been calling me nonstop for the past two days. She always calls when the holidays come around. And it's always the same thing. She wants me to come home but I can't, its too hard. I haven't been home in over three years.

"Oh, yeah. I forgot. Here, let me help." Alison smiled and handed me a box. "So how does this work? Are we just dropping off the boxes at the school or are we going to help deliver too?"

"We're actually going to deliver. I think we get to deliver to the Santa Ana shelter." Alison says

"Hey, isn't that 20 minutes from where you live, Ryan?" Kenny asks.

Oh shit. This can't be happening.

"Newport Beach is near Santa Ana?" Alison asks with a smile. I nod. "Are you going to give us a tour of your hometown?" she asks hopefully.

"When are we delivering again?" I ask trying to get out of this.

"The 22nd, tomorrow" Alison says.

"Oh, I don't think I can make it."

"What? Why? I double checked the date with you two days ago."

"I know, I just forgot" she gave me a questioning look, "I'm sorry."

She dismissed my apology and kissed my cheek, "Don't worry about it."

Alison's POV

Anna, Kenny, Corey, and I delivered the food to the shelter and spent some time there organizing the food. Corey tagged along with us because he had access to the school van, making it easier for us to deliver the food. After a couple hours, we headed home. When I arrived at the house, I saw Ryan sitting on the couch with his back turned to me. He must not have heard us enter the house because he was focused on the conversation he was having on the phone. Kenny and Anna made their way upstairs and disappeared into her bedroom.

"I just can't, Court. I'm sorry." I heard him say. Courtney is his sister. She's been calling a lot lately, but I never know why. "I don't know what else to say. I just can't okay." He sighed and ended his call.

I stood awkwardly behind him. His head hung low, and his elbows rested on his knees. He still didn't hear me walk towards him. As I walked to the side of the couch I saw him rub his forehead in frustration. I cleared my throat so he knew I was there. He looked up quickly and gave me a small smile, "Hey, when did you get in?" he asked

"Just now." He opened his arms as I sat on his lap. He held me around my waist and I brushed my fingers through his hair. He closed his eyes, "You okay?" I whispered.

He forced a smile and said, "Yeah, I'm fine." I frowned because he's been saying that a lot lately. He hasn't been himself. He tried to change the subject by asking, "How was shelter?"

"Good. We got a lot done. They said they'd be able to give the food to families in time for Thanksgiving."

I gave him a small smile and stared at his chest. I didn't know how to ask him. I wanted to know what was wrong but he never wants to talk about it. I know he's getting tired of my asking but I'm just worried about him. I looked up at him and he was looking at me. I looked into his eyes and saw sadness even though he was smiling at me.

"That's good. Who's car did you take? I noticed all your cars were here." he said

"Corey suggested he drive all of us in the school van."

He looked uncomfortable again. He always does when Corey's name is brought up. "Are you okay?"

"I'm fine." he mumbled.

"You been saying that a lot lately."

His eyes narrowed slightly as he asked, "Do you want me to say I'm jealous so you can get mad at me, again?"

"No, I don't want you to be jealous at all."

"It's not that easy, Alison. I can't just not be jealous when you're with him all the time."

I held his face in my hands and made him look at me, "I'm with you. You don't have to worry. I'm all yours."

His eyes looked like they were searching mine and he said, "I just don't want you leaving me." When he realized what he said, his eyes left mine.

"Why would you say that?" I asked him, stunned.

"Forget it." he said quickly and gently lifted me off him and stood up.

"No, why would you ever think that I'd leave you?" I asked him

He paused for a second. He opened his mouth to say something but instead he said, "Forget it, just drop it."

"No, tell me." I pleaded

"Drop it." he said sternly.

"Why won't you tell me anything? It's like you're constantly hiding things from me." He didn't answer, instead he looked away and remained silent, "Like everytime I ask you about your family, you always avoid my questions. Why can't you just talk to me?"

He sighed, "Why can't you just drop it?"

"Because I'm worried about you!" I yelled. I didn't mean to yell at him. I was getting frustrated because he wouldn't let me help him. He wouldn't let me in.

"You don't have to worry about me." he said while looking down at me. But he wasn't looking me in the eyes. He looked anywhere but in my eyes.

"I can't help it. I'm always worried about you when I see you like this. I care about you, Ryan. Don't you get it?"

He sighs and sits back down. "All I'm asking is for you to just let it go. Please?" he asks with desperation.

"I can't. Obviously this is something that is bothering you."

"But it has nothing to do with you, okay? So just let me deal with it on my own."

"Why?... Why won't you let me help you? We're together Ryan. You and me, we're an us. Let me help you."

"Us being together has nothing to do with my past. Why do you have to keep bothering me about it?"

"Because we should be able to tell each other anything. I tell you everything and you... you never tell me anything." He shook his head in frustration. "I'm just worried about you, Ryan. Lately, you've been frustrated and irritated. More than usual. And you seem sad. And I just want to know what's going on. If it has to do with me, or Corey, or your family. I want to make it better. Just tell me."

" I can't."

"I don't want to fight with you, Ryan. It hurts me when we fight. I don't like being angry with you. And if you can't tell me what's going on then how are we suppose to fix whatever's wrong?"

"I just." he sighed, "I need some time alone, is that okay?"

"What does that mean?"

"What I mean is that maybe, maybe we should cool off for a while." I didn't say anything. I just stood there staring at him until he walked out of the house. And just like that I felt empty. My heart hurt so bad I didn't even feel the tears running down my cheeks. I only realized I was crying when my vision started to blur. I can't believe it. He just... left me.

23

Chapter 22

Alison's POV

Ryan didn't even come home last night or the night before. It's been two days and he hasn't even called me. He just disappeared. I've called him a few times but after the third time I figured he didn't really care to talk to me.

"Hey" Anna says while giving me a comforting smile from across the kitchen. I've been sitting at the breakfast table for about an hour now. Just slowly eating my oatmeal. I've already cried my eyes out to her for the past two days. We've gone through all the possible reasons why Ryan had left and why he's been acting so strange but we couldn't decide on what it was. This whole thing didn't make any sense to me. The only thing that was clear was that I didn't know Ryan as well as I thought I did. These past three years, he's never once mentioned his family or anything about his past unless we asked. And we rarely asked because we saw how uncomfortable he got whenever we asked. And now, I just wish he was here so I just know he's okay. Even if he didn't want to talk, I just want him here with me. "He's fine. Don't worry, alright?"

I nodded, not fully believing her. I wouldn't believe he's okay unless I saw him. Even though I'm grateful, Anna has been here to comfort me these past couple of days, I just wanted to be home already. Having Thanksgiving dinner with my family. Then it hit me. I'll just fly home two days earlier. It'll be the first time I've ever missed class, but I didn't have any exams so it wouldn't be a big deal. I needed to be home, I needed my family. Ryan was suppose to fly home with me but I'm pretty sure that's not happening since he left me.

"I think I want to go home." I said quietly.

Anna looked shocked, "what? but you never miss class."

I sighed, "I know, but I just want to see my family. I miss them" She smiled a little, "And being home will make me feel a little better"

She nodded understanding that being with my family is something I love because we're so close.

I changed my flight date and went home the next morning to Kennebunkport, Maine. When I got home I was greeted warmly by my parents. My brother and sister were at work and my parents were retired so they were at home with my neice, Lily, and nephew, James. I helped babysit. When the little ones were asleep for their daytime nap I went to the backyard and sat on the swinging bench. I loved being home. I loved reminiscing about growing up in this house with my brother and sister. But this time, being home didn't feel the same. I thought being home would help me feel better but I was still worrying about Ryan. By now, I was frustrated with him. First, he wouldn't talk to me, then he wouldn't let me help him, then he just left, then he didn't even answer my phone calls making me worry about him even more. Why does he do this to me? I HATE WORRYING ABOUT HIM. I hate this feeling. I hate seeing him hurt. I hate not being able to help him. Why does he make me feel this way?

My dad walks out unto the backyard and walks towards me and takes a seat next to me. "How's my munchkin doing?" he asks as he pulls me into a side hug. I rest my head on his shoulder.

"I'm okay." I sigh as my mom joins us and sits on the other side.

He lets out a chuckle, "Now, I know that's not true. What's the matter?"

"I just missed you guys."

"We missed you too. But I know you love school and your friends over there. You know, your mom and I love having you home, but you almost never come home early. Is something wrong? Did you have a fight with Anna? or Ryan?" My eyes begin to fill with tears, "Say, isn't that boyfriend of yours suppose to be here?" Tears begin to fall and I sniff. My dad notices and he releases me from the hug to look at me. "Oh honey, what is it?"

"That boyfriend of mine." I blubber, "He-he-, he left me"

"What? Now, why would he do that?" my mom asks as she runs her fingers through my hair soothingly.

"I don't know!" I whine. "First we were arguing about him being jealous then it shifted into him not telling me things. Then I told him he never tells me anything, like things about his family. Then I asked him to just tell me and he said he can't. Then he said that he needed some time alone and that we should cool off. What does that even mean? And then he left. He just left." I said it all too fast. My dad, looking a little confused tried to replay what I just blurted out in his head. "How could he just leave me?"

"I don't know. But it seems like he's struggling with some things right now." my dad says.

"I know he is, but why won't he just let me help him?" I ask throwing my hands in the air.

"Honey." my mom says soothingly as she wipes my tears with her delicate fingers, "Some people just need time."

"How much time?"

She smiles and brushes a stray piece of hair away from my tear stained face, "Depends. But if he's as wonderful as you described, he'll come around. I'm sure of it."

"I just want him to be okay. I don't want him to hurt." I say as I look down at my hands and add "And I really miss him"

"Oh Patrick, she's in love." my mom says to my dad.

"Don't tell me I'm going to have to give another daughter away so soon. I'm already giving one away this weekend." My dad says.

My head shoots up and I look at her, then at my dad. In love? This is what being in love feels like? Is it suppose to hurt this bad?

Ryan's POV

I take a deep breath before knocking on my sister's front door. She's the only person that could even begin to understand what was going through my head. I haven't been home in over 3 years. Newport beach hasn't changed much since then. The weather was still warm despite the fact that winter was approaching; typical Southern California weather.

My sister swung the door open and looked shocked for a split second but it quickly changed into indifference, "Hi. May I help you?" she asked nonchalantly.

"Court, come on." I groaned

"I'm sorry, do I know you?" she asked sarcastically.

"Yeah. I'm your little brother... Ryan, does that name ring a bell?"

"Hmm... not really." then she attempted to close the door. I don't blame her for acting this way. Once I left Newport, I never looked back. I would keep in touch with her, but I never came home.

I kept her from closing the door, "Court, please? I need to talk to you. I'm a fucking mess right now and I left my girlfriend crying because I couldn't talk to her. I need your help. Please?" I begged her.

She sighed dramatically and finally held the door open for me. I walked into her house. I've only been here once when I helped her and her husband Jack move in four years ago. It definitely looked like a home. They put pictures up on every wall. We both sat on the couch. I was trying to get myself to ask for her help but a pillow hit me on the side of the head before I could say anything.

"Court, what the hell?" I yell as the pillow falls limp on the carpet beneath my feet.

My sister always knew how to put me in my place. I haven't seen her in 3 years and she's still the same. The same older sister that bosses me around, annoys the hell out of me, and gives me great advice even when I don't ask for it.

"That's for not visiting us. And this.." she slaps me on the back of the head, "is for making that girlfriend of yours, cry." Shit, she still slaps as hard as I remember. Maybe even harder. I rubbed the back of my skull to ease the pain but it was throbbing. "How could you just leave her crying? I thought you actually care about this one?"

"I don't know. It's the first time I've ever made her cry."

"I should hit you again." She raised her hand and I flinched, "but I won't. You look like you're hurting enough."

"Thanks."

"So you're here because you need me to help you stop being a sucky boyfriend?" she teased but she realized it was serious when I wasn't making smart ass remarks back to her.

"I'm terrified she's going to leave me. I know she would never do anything to intentionally hurt me but in the back of my mind I always feel like she's going to be swept off her feet by someone else. Like..."

"Like mom." I nod

"What if she leaves me like mom left us? I'd fall apart, Court. Just like dad did. Mom left him, and he killed himself"

"But Alison's not like mom. You know that. You can't spend your life being afraid that everyone is going to leave."

"But everyone does leave."

"I've always been here, Ryan."

"I try so hard to convince myself that Alison's not like her. But I just get really jealous and crazy when she's spending time with any other guy but me." I paused, "Because what if she ends up falling for that other guy and decides she doesn't want to be with me anymore. If my own parents can't stay for me, why would she?"

Her face softened, "Ryan, you've spent so long running away from what happened instead of dealing with it." I didn't deny it, she was right. When my mom left, I didn't talk about it with anyone. I was angry, hurt, sad, and it showed despite how hard I tried to hide it. I watched my dad fall into depression. He would come home drunk almost every night. He quit his job and when he finally couldn't take it anymore, he killed himself. He ran his car off a cliff. He didn't even care that he was leaving me all alone. I was almost 18 when he died but I was still in high school. Courtney was away for college. She took a semester off to stay with me while I finished high school. She would constantly try to get me to talk to her, but I didn't want to. I hated talking about it because it would just bring back feelings that I hate feeling. Over time, I just stopped being angry, I forgot about being sad, and I didn't realize I was still hurt. When I moved away for college, I busied myself with everything just so I wouldn't have to remember my past, my family, my home, and my parents. And it worked. I never went home to visit. I met Kenny, then Alison and Anna. I made my own new family and forgot about my old one. I didn't know that it would catch up with me. I didn't think that I'd have mommy issues. "You took it the hardest. None of us really knew what to do. You wouldn't let us help you. You just shut everyone out and left the second you had a chance to. And now, everything is coming back. Maybe it's time to finally deal with it."

"I don't know how to."

"I'll help you. And you should let Alison help you too. If you shut her out, you might lose her too."

24

Chapter 23

Ryan's POV

"You must be Ryan", Alison's mom said to me when she opened the door. I recognized her from all the pictures Alison had up in her room. Alison looked a lot like her. They had the same grey eyes and dark brown hair. But Alison was probably a good 5 inches shorter.

"Yes, Mrs. Stewart."

"Please, call me Sandra." She said with a smile. She probably doesn't know about the fight Alison and I had, or else she wouldn't be this nice to me.

"Honey, Katelynn's asking what to add to the stuffing." Alison's dad says to Sandra as he walks into the foyer. This man was huge. He looked like he could pick me up and throw me to Mars without a problem. He was probably four inches taller than me. Since I'm already six foot, he's 6'4. How did Alison end up so small? He smiles at me and extends his hand to shake mine, "I'm Patrick, you must be Ryan." I took his hand in mine and shook it.

"Yes, Sir."

"Please, call me Patrick." He said immediately. "You must be here for Alison."

I nod, "Yeah, I am. Can I please speak to her?"

"Of course you can. I'm so glad you could make it." Sandra says. She takes a look at my one bag and says, "You should put that upstairs."

"Oh, I'm not sure that Alison would want that. You see..."

Before I could finish what I was saying, Sandra says, "Oh sweetie, she may be angry right now, but she'll hear you out."

"Wait, you know about our fight?"

She nods with a smile, "We do and I think you two will be able to work through whatever the problem is. Our daughter seems to care about you a lot and since you're here, you probably care about her too."

"I do. I need explain some things to her." I said quietly.

"Well, then let's go get her." Her mom says, still smiling. How is she so understanding about everything?

We walk through the foyer and enter the opening to the living room. I see Alison sitting on a rug near their coffee table. She has her back facing me. She's playing with an infant that couldn't be more than 2 years old. They were watching some children's program. Alison was holding both of the child's hands in hers and moving them to the beat of the song. Alison sang along as the child tried to sing too. The child giggled.

"Munchkin, you have a visitor." Her dad says to her.

"Who is –" She says as she turns to face me. Her smile faded once she saw me. She stood up with the child in her arms and said, "I'll be back, Lily." The child gives her a sloppy kiss and Alison smiles in return.

Her mom takes Lily and Alison doesn't look at me but instead says, "Follow me."

We walked up the stairs and entered what I'm assuming is her room. Right when she closed the door she started to slap me on my chest multiple times. "How could you just leave me like that? Do you have any idea how worried I've been about you? How could you make me feel like that?" I let her slap me. She was angry at me, and she had a right to be. Her voice became quieter and quieter as I wrapped my arms around her. She stopped slapping me. She didn't push me away nor did she hug me back, she just let me hold her. "You just left me, Ryan." She cried into my chest.

"I know" I whispered, "I shouldn't have just walked out on you. I'm sorry. I've been such a shitty boyfriend lately and you deserve better. I promise to be better if you'll let me."

She pulled away from me and crossed her arms over her chest. Then I saw it. The pain in her eyes, looks so much like my dad's when my mom left. I'm no better than my mom. I hurt my girlfriend; I left Alison and hurt her. "Why should I?"

"Because I'm in love with you and I can't lose you"

She looked at me long and hard with glassy eyes before she said, "No you don't. If you loved me you would've never left. You would have let me in. When you love someone, you tell them everything. And you don't do any of those things so how could you love me? Do you even know what love is?"

"I don't know the exact definition of love, but I do know that I love you."

She narrowed her eyes and asked, "How do you know?"

"Because when I see you crying like you are right now, all I want to do is make you smile again. Because you're the only girl I can even begin to picture a future with. And because when I'm not with you I'm a complete mess. I don't know how else to explain it but every moment I spend with you just reaffirms that you're the only girl I want to spend the rest of my life with."

Her face softened as I continued, "I never thought that I'd feel this way. I never thought that I could love someone as much as I love you. When I first met you, I knew that I'd fall for you, but I didn't expect to feel like this. I didn't expect to love everything about you... your beautiful eyes, your breathtaking smile, your flawless face, and your soft hair."

She shifted slightly and I took a step closer to her, "I love that you care so much about me. I love that you're genuine, sweet, and kind. I love how every time feels like the first time with you. I love the way you ramble when you're nervous. I love how perfectly you fit in my arms. I love the way you smell. I love how you're such a nerd sometimes. I love the way you play with my fingers. I love how you trust me. And I absolutely love that we're best friends."

She bit down on her bottom lip to keep from smiling, "I didn't expect to love the way you make me feel, when you hold my hand, when you look at me, or when you brush your fingers through my hair. I still can't explain it. You make me so happy. You mean everything to me."

Her lips parted ever so slightly and she was looking at me like I was her world. I wiped away her tears with my thumbs and said, "That's how I know."

She smiled through her tears and she brought her hands up to my face and pulled me down to kiss her. Not being able to touch her, feel her, kiss her for three days was torture. Once her lips met mine, I couldn't help but pull her whole body against mine. I needed her. We kissed and kissed until we were gasping for air. "I love you so much, Alison." I said sounding breathless.

I felt her smile against my lips and she kissed me once more, "I love you too."

Alison's POV

"I missed you so much." I whispered as he rested his forehead against mine. I opened my eyes and he had his closed still.

He opened his eyes and pulled away slightly to look at me, "I missed you too. I'm never leaving you again, I promise"

I looked at him carefully before asking, "Where did you go?"

He sighed, grabbed a hold on my hand and led me to my bed. He sat down and I sat on his lap. He looked tired. I brushed my fingers through his hair, his eyes fluttered closed. Then he slowly opens his eyes to look at me. He gives me a small smile and says, "I went home to see my sister. After our fight, I needed someone to talk to and the only person that would begin to understand is my sister. When we were fighting, a lot of things were going through my head. Things from my past that I haven't told anyone about, things that I hate talking about because of the way it makes me feel. And when I realized that the reason why I've been acting so jealous was because I'm afraid of losing you everything just came crashing together. My past and you. I didn't realize that my past was affecting the way I am with you."

"What happened?"

He exhaled deeply and said quietly, "My mom's not dead... when I was thirteen my mom left me, my dad and my sister. She left us for her student in her dance class. She didn't even leave a note, she took all her things and just left. She never came back. I waited months thinking she would come back. But she didn't." His eyes were filled with hurt and I couldn't help but hurt too. "I watched my dad fall apart. He was depressed and he turned to alcohol. He just gave up on everything, including me. And when I was 17 he decided that he had nothing else to live for. He killed himself. Courtney helped me as much as she could. She even put off school to stay with me in Newport until I graduated. She even offered to stay. She was always there for me but I just pushed her away. I didn't want to talk about it... with anyone. I just wanted to get away from all of it. I didn't want to remember anything that happened. So I just left Newport once I got accepted to UCSD. When I got to UCSD, it was like a fresh start, like a new beginning for me. It was just easier for me to say that my mom passed away. I didn't mean to lie to you guys, I just couldn't have people feel bad for me. Back home, I was embarrassed and felt ashamed, neglected, and pathetic. My own parents couldn't even stay for me. Everyone back home knew about it and I just wanted to forget it ever happened. But apparently I can't run away from it. When I said that I don't want you to leave me, it hit me. I have mommy issues. I'm so messed up. You're best thing that's ever happened to me. You're always there for me and all I do is push you away. I push everyone away. I'm so messed up."

He looked down but I made him look at me. I took his face between my hands and said clearly, "You're not messed up... you're amazing. After everything you've been through, you've managed to grow up into such an incredible man who I'm proud to call my boyfriend. And I love you so much, Ryan. Your parents were selfish for leaving you but what they did has done nothing but turn you into who are you right now. You're selfless, caring, sweet, kind, ambitious, loving... I can go on and on. You are the furthest thing from messed up." He gave me a weak smile, "You're perfect, and you're all mine."

He softly kissed me before saying, "I'm so lucky to have you."

"You'll always have me." I told him, "Remember that, okay?"

His eyes didn't leave mine. They bore into mine, they weren't searching, they were just piercing through. I could tell he fully believed me. There wasn't any doubt. He was sure that I would be there for him. And without hesistation he said, "Okay."

Chapter 24

Ryan's POV

I arrived at Alison's house right when Thanksgiving dinner was about happen. Alison introduced me to her sister Katelynn and her fiancé Tom, her brother Matthew and his wife Michelle and their children Chase, James and baby Lily. While we ate dinner, I was really nervous. I came here with everyone already knowing that Alison and I had a fight before hand and I was just preparing myself for the tough questioning but it never came. The conversation at the dinner table was surprisingly easy. They were open and easy to talk to.

It was late and the kids all fell asleep. All the adults settled in the living room with coffee. Everyone had there own little conversations going on until it was time to get grilled. I knew it was coming…

"So Ryan, you seem like a perfectly sane young man." Sandra said, "What about our Alison could you possibly like?"

"Oh here we go." Alison rolled her eyes, clearly aware of where her mom was going with this conversation. I gave her a questioning look and she smiled and whispered, "Just wait for it."

"I mean, she's an awful cook." Sandra said seriously.

"She's a dwarf." Katelynn added.

"She's a nerd" Matthew said quickly after.

And finally, Patrick said, "And don't forget how big of a neat freak she is."

I had no idea what was going on. I looked all around and they all had serious expressions on their faces. It was quiet and Sandra asked, "How could you possibly like a tiny, nerdy, neat freak who can't cook?"

I look to Alison and she's just smirking at me. And I say, "I just do. Actually, I love all those things about her."

It was silent for a moment. Then Patrick said, "Great answer."

Then Katelynn's fiancé, Tom says, "Damn, I was panicking when you guys ambushed me like that."

They all laugh as Sandra says, "Oh I'm sorry, Ryan. We just couldn't help ourselves. You're the first boy Alison's brought home."

"They've done it to all my boyfriends." Katelynn says.

"And to all my girlfriends. So it was only fair for us to pull it on you." Matt says.

They all laughed and my brows furrowed in confusion. Alison explained, "It all started when Matt brought this girl home, I don't even remember her name. But anyways, Matt repeatedly begged us to not embarrass him." Matt shook his head while chuckling, "But we just couldn't resist. Mom, Dad, Katelynn and I devised a plan to bring up embarrassing things about Matt and make the girl nervous. It was originally for laughs but it turned into a Stewart family tradition. So now, we put all the new girlfriends and boyfriends in the hot seat and see if they can handle it."

"Yeah and that girl really couldn't handle it." Katelynn laughs.

"Poor girl was practically running out the front door. I actually felt bad." Alison says

"But that didn't stop the tradition." Matt says

"Nope," Alison laughed, "It wasn't just for laughs, I promise."

"No, it wasn't. It quickly turned into a test that determined whether or not the girl or guy was right for our kids." Sandra said

"What does it take to pass?" I asked

Patrick looked at his wife Sandra then back at me, "Well, I guess they pass if they care about our kids enough to deal with us... the crazy Stewart family."

"I passed with flying colors." Michelle declares

"I passed...barely." Tom says quietly. Everyone bursts out laughing and Tom explains, "What? I was nervous."

Alison turns to me and says, "And you, passed too. So that means, you're right for me too."

Once everyone went home, Alison's parents had me settled into the guest room down the hall from Alison's room. They knew Alison and I lived in the same house but I guess they didn't think we slept together. Her dad made it clear that we were to sleep in separate rooms. As much as I would love to have her in my arms tonight, I completely understand why he didn't want us sleeping in the same room.

Alison's POV

Black Friday, the day after Thanksgiving is something the girls in the family look forward to every year. Shopping. Shopping. Shopping. I love this time of year. I go shopping with my mom and Katelynn every year and this year was no exception. And I know that leaving Ryan with my dad and the guys seems like it would be scary situation for him but he seems to be getting along great with the guys. In fact, he fits right in. I knew my family would love him. So, I went shopping in the city with my mom and Katelynn and the guys stayed at my parents house with the kids.

Like every Black Friday, We have dinner at my parents house. After dinner, Ryan and I do the dishes and I glance over at my brother Matt and his wife Michelle and smile to myself. They've been married for 10 years and I swear they still look at each other like they did back when they were dating. They got married when they were eighteen. Most people would automatically predict that they wouldn't last but here they are... 10 years later and still going strong. They have three beautiful children, they work through most of the day and they come home with their kids. They don't have time to themselves and I think that they deserve some time alone.

While rinsing the plate Ryan hands me, I nudge his elbow with mine, "Hey" He raises his eyebrow questioningly "What do you say to some awesome babysitting, tonight?"

"What?" He laughs

"I think Matt and Michelle deserve a night off"

He looks over at the married couple, then their three children bouncing around, and looks hesitantly at me, "I don't know the first thing about babysitting."

"You aren't doing this alone. We're a team. I'll help you." I clasp my rubber gloved hands together and pout, "Please? Pretty please?"

He rolls his eyes and kisses my nose, "Fine, but I'm not changing diapers."

"Deal!"

After dessert, Katelynn and Tom head home and my parents have already turned in for the night. Though it took a bit of convincing, Matt and Michelle agreed to have a night off and leave the kids with

Ryan and me. I've babysat for them before but never Chase, James and Lily at the same time. But I'm almost positive Ryan and I can handle it.

From 8 to 9 o'clock, Chase and James seemed to be on sugar highs because of the ice cream they had for dessert. They were bouncing around like crazy. But thankfully the sugar wore off and now James was starting to doze off and Chase was busy playing COD with Ryan in the living room. All the while, Lily was napping in the spare bedroom that use to be Matt's room. My parents quickly turned his room into a extra room for their grandchildren so that they'd always have a place in the house.

Getting Chase to go to bed was easy and now Ryan and I are officially off duty and relaxing on the couch. Ryan lets out a deep breath.

"That wasn't so bad was it?" I ask

He chuckles, "No, it wasn't. But that first hour was really tough."

"I know... now we know why parents don't like to give their children sugar."

"I don't know how Matt and Michelle do it."

"They've had years of practice."

"But they're good kids." I nod "Really well behaved ... after the sugar wears off."

A moment of silence passed before he added, "And now, the kids are asleep, and we're here... on this cozy couch... all alone..."

He scooted over to me before giving me a cheeky grin and leaning in to give me a kiss. And right before our lips meet we hear Lily crying. We both head upstairs and once I get to Lily I quickly try to lull her back to sleep. But it isn't working. And I just remember that it was time to feed her. I had to get her bottle ready.

I try to hand Lily to Ryan but he backs away with his hands pushing air between us, "What's the problem?" I laugh

"I've never held a baby before." He said looking terrified

"Oh come on, she's not a monster."

"No, she's not... she's quite adorable but I'm positive she'll cry even more if I held her."

"No she won't, just hold her for a minute. I need to get her bottle ready." He gave me an unsure look but gave in. He carefully took her in his arms and tried his best to soothe her, "I'll be back in a minute, I promise."

I hurry off to the kitchen and prepare her bottle faster than I thought I could and run up the stairs. As I approach the room I hear Ryan singing Twinkle, Twinkle, Little Star. I couldn't help but smile. I tiptoed to the room and found myself watching my boyfriend sing to my baby niece. At that moment my heart melted, I can't even explain how cute he looked. He was singing in hushed tones while gently swaying with Lily in his arms. Just as he turns in my direction he sees me smiling at him and he stops singing.

"Keep singing" I whisper.

Twinkle, twinkle, little star

How I wonder what you are

Baby Lily is sound asleep and I help him place her back in her crib. Right when Lily is placed in the crib she stirs a bit and Ryan immediately prepares himself to pick her up again, "Oh no, she's waking up." He whispers, worried that she'll cry again.

"She's fine, she's sound asleep. All thanks to you." I say to him as he tugs me by the waist towards him, "You're an awesome babysitter."

He chuckles, "We're awesome babysitters... we're a team, remember?"

"A team", I nod

He smiles that breathtaking smile I love so much and kisses me. After the fight, I never thought that everything between Ryan and I would be this great. We hit a low when we fought that night and after he finally told me about his fear and his past we've just gotten closer. I'm seeing a side of him that I've never seen before. A side that's vulnerable and it may sound silly but I'm seeing a side that's more grown up and mature. A side I really love. I've never been able to picture my future with Ryan as clearly as I can now. Before, I knew that Ryan and I could have a future together but I've never been able to picture any of it in my head. Now, it's easier to see us being married, having a family together, and growing old together.

CHAPTER 25

Ryan's POV

"Ry" I hear my girlfriend whisper as I feel her warm hand sweep across my cheek. I slowly open my eyes and blink to adjust my vision. She smiles, "Get dressed, I want to show you something."

I look over at the alarm clock on the nightstand and it was 7:30AM, "This early?" I yawn.

She laughed quietly, "Mhm. I have a lot stuff planned for us today. So, time to get up, boyfriend"

So, I got up and got dressed. We met downstairs and found ourselves with matching outfits. We both had on jeans and a black pea coat. Talk about a cheesy couple. She noticed the matching situation and said, "Copy cat."

We headed out the front door and starting walking down the neighborhood streets. I had no idea what we were doing today. All she told me was that she was going to give me a tour of her hometown.

The weather was cold and gloomy compared to warm and sunny California. But the gloom couldn't diminish the beauty of this town. Kennebunkport, Maine is a different kind of beautiful. This small town is simple, warm, and dare I say it... cute. Just like Alison. The little shops and cafes were family owned. The grocery shops didn't have bar scanners, just old cash registers. The people were warm and friendly; they treat you like family. They are just genuinely nice people. I can honestly say I've never seen or been to a place like this.

She took me to her elementary school and showed me where she had her first job. She worked as a waitress at a local family restaurant called Dally's, which was where we had lunch. Then she took me to the Welcome to Kennebunkport sign and told me I had to take pictures with the sign because I'm a first time visitor. We took goofy couple pictures in front of the sign. The tour ended at a nearby playground. She told me countless stories about the adventures she had with her brother and sister as we climbed onto the jungle gym. We sat on the edge with our legs dangling in the air. I pulled her closer to me as she rested her head on my shoulder. The cold air didn't feel as cold now. A comfortable silence took over before she said while looking into the distance, "We're all grown up now."

"What makes you say that?"

She sighed, "I don't know. It might be my sister getting married. Because, just a few years ago she was graduating from college just like me and now she's getting married, starting the rest of her life with Tom."

"Well, we're not officially grown up yet. We still have 7 months till then."

"Okay, but we're growing up. We're going to graduate soon and start working. Then next thing comes marriage and kids. I can still remember running across this playground, how can we be grown up now?"

"Don't you want to grow up? I can totally picture you being a great teacher and an awesome wife and mom."

She looks at me smirking, "Can you now?"

"Oh, don't act like you weren't thinking about marrying me", I tease.

Her smile widens, "But I wasn't."

"You so were."

"Even if I was, it's not going to happen until we're officially grown up."

"Oh fine, then I guess we're saving that whole marrying each other thing until after graduation. Agreed?"

I held my hand out to seal the deal and she shook it, "Agreed." She smiled and asked in panic, "Oh my god, what time is it?"

I checked my watch, "3:30, should we be heading back?"

"Yeah, Kate and I are getting our hair and make up done at 4:15."

"Oh, are you going to look for hair and make up ideas for our big day?", I joked.

"Ha, ha", she said sarcastically.

"What? Oh, sorry. Are we at the part where we talk about our kids running around this playground?" She shoots me a playful glare before I say, "Oh right, we're not there yet."

"Nope, not yet."

"Then, I guess the only thing we have left to do for these next seven months is be kids. And I think we can start by playing tag."

She smiled widely and said, "I think that's a good idea, but we have to leave in 10 minutes. And not it!" Then she took off running to go down the slide.

Alison's POV

Kate, the rest of the bridesmaids, the maid of honor and I finished getting ready and headed to the church. Once we got there, we had five minutes to wait before we can enter the sanctuary.

"I'm getting married" my beautiful sister says smiling widely.

"You are, and I'm so so happy for you, Kate."

Her eyes became glassy as she said, "Thank you so much for always being there for me. Thanks for helping me out with the wedding stuff." I try to dismiss her thank you's because I'd do anything for her but she just kept going, "No, you live all the way in California and you still helped out so much. You're the best little sister in the world. A-and" by now tears were escaping her eyes, "I'm so happy for you too. You deserve to be happy and I'm glad Ryan makes you happy."

Now, my eyes were tearing up. "Aw Kate, you're the best big sister anyone could have. Now, please stop crying, you're going to ruin your makeup. "

"And yours too, apparently." she laughed through her tears.

We took a bunch of deep breaths and prepared ourselves to walk down the aisle. We heard the organ begin to play and I walked down the aisle and saw Ryan sitting in the second pew. Once he saw the ridiculously fluffy pink bridesmaid gown I was wearing he raised his eyebrows, smiled and gave me a thumbs up.

The ceremony was beautiful. And now it was time for the reception.

Ryan and I were slow dancing when he said, "Describe your ideal wedding."

"This may surprise you, but I haven't really thought about it."

"Really?"

I nod, "I guess I just focused on the kind of guy I'd be marrying."

"And what kind of guy would that be?" he asked

"He would have to be someone I have share everything with. Someone I can laugh with, someone who I'll be excited to spend everyday with." He smiles broadly while I add, "Why, what would your ideal wedding be like?"

He pretended to think, "Hmm, well it would have to be in your hometown. Your family would have to be there. And you'd have to be standing at the altar opposite me. Exchanging vows with me. Saying I do with me."

At the playground we were joking about getting married and having kids and now we're doing the same thing, except now he seem a little more serious, like he actually meant what he was saying.

He sets my bags down on the floor near my bed as I collapse back first onto my bed from exhaustion, "We're finally home."

He chuckles as he sits beside my limp body and looks over his shoulder at me, "Are you really that exhausted?"

I nod.

He laughs, "But you slept the whole time we were on the plane."

"There's something about plane rides that wear me out." He shakes his head and smiles. He falls back so that we're lying down side by side. I turn my body towards his as he turns his towards mine. He gives me a warm smile before I say, "Thanks for doing the whole meet the family thing."

"I loved every minute of it."

"You did?"

He nods, "Your family is just as amazing as you described. Being around them this weekend put a lot of things in perspective for me."

I sat up and he did the same, "Yeah? Like what?"

He smiled and swept my hair behind my ear, "Well, like... now I know I want to spend the rest of my life with you, marry you, have a family with you, have everything with you."

"Wow, all that, huh?"

He nods. He's smiling, and it's not that smile he has when he's joking. It's that sincere smile. He's actually being serious about us getting married and having a family. I'm not just imagining this, right?

"I love you", he whispers softly.

And that moment my eyes couldn't leave his. I just wanted to get closer to him. He kissed me tenderly. I couldn't hear it but I whispered I love you against his lips. He continued to kiss me softly. It was slow and passionate. I was trying to memorize each movement his lips made against mine. It's like I knew something special was going to happen. He gently pulls me onto his lap. My hands involuntarily started to unbutton his shirt. And once I finished with the last button his lips separated from mine. I opened my eyes to find him studying my face. My fingers grazed the smooth skin on his chest. I slipped his shirt off his broad shoulders. Once his shirt was off, I let my hands explore and my eyes followed. I ran my hands up his muscular arms, down his chest to his rock hard abs. I returned my eyes back to his. He was waiting. Waiting to see how far I was going to go. His hands remained on my hips. I kissed him slowly and pulled away slightly.

I looked at him and with his eyes still closed he asked, "Is this really happening?"

I couldn't help but smile. He opened his eyes and I nodded. His right hand caressed my cheek and he gently held my face as he kissed me. This was perfect.

Chapter 26

Ryan's POV

I flip the pancake and feel two arms wrap around my middle from behind. It's Alison. I feel her tiptoe and kiss the back of my neck.

"Someone's finally up." I tell her.

She giggles into my back, "It's only 9."

"Well, I've been up for hours, slaving over this hot stove, making us breakfast."

"Slaving? Please, you love cooking. Especially when you're cooking for me."

I turn around and place the finished pancake on the already tall stack of pancakes. She beams at me, "You're right. I love cooking for you. Especially when you come down in your cute little pajamas ready to eat."

She smiles, "How'd you know I was hungry?"

"You're always hungry."

She sticks her tongue at me before we sit down to eat. As she cuts through a short stack of pancakes she asks me, "Have you heard from Kenny and Anna?"

I shook my head

She took a sip of her tea before she said, "I'm worried. They didn't come home last night. You think something happened to them?"

"They've been M.I.A before. I'm sure they're okay. Don't worry. And I'm kind of glad they didn't come home last night. Who knows what they would have seen or heard."

A faint shade of pink fills the skin on her cheeks as I reminded her of what happened last night. It was our first time. I will never forget the noises that she made, the way she held onto me, and the way she looked at me last night.

She was looking at me from under her eyelashes, looking extremely sexy. I was more than ready to repeat what we did last night when the front door opens and Kenny and Anna walk in the house looking all bright eyed and happy. Alison immediately runs up to them to smother them in her arms. In all my life, I've never seen a friend like Alison. She's the best friend any one can have. She's been worrying about Kenny and Anna since last night. I walked over to my friends and welcomed them back.

"Alison, please tell me you haven't been worrying about us." Anna says to Alison.

"Of course I have, you two were suppose to be here last night. I thought you two were spending Thanksgiving here this year."

"We were suppose to be here but we just had to see Anna's parents." Kenny says.

Kenny and Anna were being extremely vague. They were oddly excited about something that Alison and I didn't know about. Alison and I both looked at each other, clearly confused about what was going on.

"Will you two please tell us what's going on?" Alison asks impatiently.

Anna and Kenny sit on the couch and ask us to join them. Alison and I slowly take our seats and nervously wait for them to tell us.

Anna takes a deep breath before she says, "I'm pregnant."

Alison and I were at a loss for words. I can't tell you what was going through her mind but she was clearly in shock. And so was I. Anna and Kenny are two 21-year olds. Anna is still in her last year of college and Kenny has just started his business. They haven't really started their lives yet and they have a baby on the way. I was worried for them, but they looked like they were prepared to take on this challenge. They've made up their minds about what they were going to do. You can tell, by just looking at them that they want this.

"Ohmygod, why didn't you tell me?" Alison asks still in shock.

"We just didn't want to ruin your time at home. With Ryan meeting your family and your sister's wedding. I just didn't want to interrupt anything that you might have been going on." Anna explains

"You're so ridiculous. You could come to me with anything. Especially something like this!" Alison began, "Anna, you're pregnant. You're going to be a mom." She says smiling widely as she makes her way to Anna to give her a big hug.

Anna begins to tear up happily, "I know. I can't believe it. I mean, I know it's crazy. We haven't thought everything through yet but we know this is what we want." She looks at Kenny and he holds her hand comfortingly, "We've always talked about getting married and having kids someday. I guess someday is now."

I congratulate my two good friends. As crazy as all this seems, I'm happy as long as they're happy.

Alison's POV

So much has happened this past week. I've realized that I love Ryan more than I ever thought I could. He's shown me sides of himself I haven't seen all three years we've known each other. And now Anna's pregnant. She and Kenny are so excited about having a family. And now everything just seems so real. My future with Ryan couldn't be any clearer. I had my head on his chest while he had his arm wrapped around my midsection. I was staring blankly at my bedroom wall when he asked, "What are you thinking about?"

I pull myself up as he gripped onto me, "So I know we were joking around about getting married and having kids together but last night when you said that you wanted everything with me, did you mean it?"

Without hesitation he said, "I did."

"It would be okay if you aren't entirely sure. I love you and I want you to know that you don't have to say those things just because you know its what I want to hear. And..."

He interrupted me with a kiss, "Stop." I just stared at him, "I meant every word. I think I knew I wanted all those things with you for a long time, I just didn't realize it until this weekend." He stared at me for a moment before he said, "Hold on..." then he went to my desk and came back with a black sharpie marker.

"What are you going to do with that?" I asked

He smiled and took my left hand, "This is to show you that I meant every word." He began to draw on my ring finger, "I want to spend the rest of my life with you and that includes getting married and having a family together. I want to be your husband someday. I want to have kids with you... a daughter that looks exactly like you or a son that looks like me but with your eyes. A future with you is exactly what I want." He finished and presented a neatly drawn ring around my finger. "There."

I looked at the black ring around my finger as he said, "I know it's just marker but means just as much as one of those things..." he was so cute he didn't know what it was called.

"A promise ring?"

He nodded, "Yeah, a promise ring. I drew it on the right hand right?"

I laughed, "Yeah, you did. I love it."

I held his face between my hands and kissed him again and again.

28

Chapter 27

5 months later...

ALISON'S POV

"Just tell me already!" I whine for the hundredth time. He just laughs and continues to drive to wherever he was taking me. "Ryan, please?" He shakes his head, "When will you just give in and tell me?"

"Never", he smiles. "I'm going to keep giving you surprises till we're old and grey and unable to walk."

He wasn't budging. I already knew he wasn't going to tell me but I can't help but try to get him to tell me. I just get so excited and anxious. He has been extremely secretive about where he has been and what he's been doing lately. I would catch him whispering into his cell phone. I've caught glimpses of some of his conversations. A lot of it sounded like business transactions. And when I asked what he was doing he'd just smile and say, "You'll see." Every time those two words were said to me, it killed me. The anticipation was unbearable. Now, two weeks later I finally get to see what he has been up to.

He shoots me yet another brilliant smile as he takes my hand in his and brings it to his lips to place a sweet kiss on it, "Patience is key Miss Stewart."

We pull up into an empty parking lot of what looks like an old run down restaurant and bar. There wasn't much light. The street lights were the only light source illuminating the area. It was dim and I just couldn't help but wonder why his surprises took place in the dark. We parked and he came around to my side of the car and opened the door for me. As he helped me out of the car I took another look at the abandoned building and suddenly saw something familiar. The large windows... they had a very familiar flower design on the glass. I've seen it before, but I couldn't remember where I've seen it. I try to link these windows to my memory but I just can't figure out where I am.

"I've been here before" I tell him.

He doesn't say anything. He just continues to escort me to the entrance. He reaches into his pocket to retrieve a set of keys. He unlocks the knob and opens the door. The door slowly swings open with a slight creak. He reaches for my hand and slips his fingers between mine. We step inside and he switches the lights on. And immediately I remember. I look back and he just gives me that adorable boyish smile. He takes my hand and leads me further inside, all the while glancing back to see the reaction on my face. I can't quite tell you what my face looked like but I'm sure it had a mixture of surprise and awe. I couldn't help but lose my breath when I saw what was before me. We were at Randy's. This is where I first met him. It looked about the same except it was empty. All the tables, chairs and booths weren't there. But there were twinkling lights all around the room hanging from the ceiling. It was beautiful. It reminded me of our first date.

"This is where I first met you." He finally said as he led me to the far right corner of the room and slowly walked backward away from me, still looking at me, "You were standing right there in this frilly crème colored top with a simple pair of blue skinny jeans and flats sipping on some red colored drink. I had no idea who you were, I just knew that the moment I walked into the room I just saw you. And you were beautiful."

By now he was at the entrance just gazing at me from across the room. Then he started walking back towards me, "Then Kenny started walking in your direction and for some odd reason I was a little disappointed because I thought you'd be the Anna he had been talking about. And if you were his Anna, he and I would have had a little problem because I knew that I was attracted to you. But the moment Anna said, 'this is my roommate Alison' I was so relieved."

He shook my hand, his eyes never leaving mine. "Even then I was drawn to you. You know the saying, 'When we first met, I had no idea you would be so important to me?' Well… I knew. I knew you'd be the most important thing to me, even if I didn't want you to be, and even if I wasn't ready and willing for you to be. And even though I never cared to show interest in any girls I've met before you, I just wanted to know you. I wanted to know what made you smile that pretty smile of yours. I wanted to know what it was about you that drew me in. We talked the whole night. I never thought I could have such a magnetic attraction to anyone. But with you, it was easy. Before then, I couldn't remember laughing so hard or smiling so big. Then I got to walk you home. You would talk about the most random things."

He smiled to himself, "It was cute. And you know what I loved most about that walk?" he asked.

"What?" I said.

His eyes bore through mine, "The way your eyes lit up whenever you told me something about your family. A lot of people would think that talking about one's family with someone they had just met is strange or odd but I liked it. A lot of people made me feel like I missed out on having a real family, but you made me feel like I didn't. Like I was a part of your family, the kind of family I've always wanted. You made me think that I still had a chance to have that family I've always wanted. I needed someone like you to help me realize that. And I'm so grateful to have met you and to have you now. That first day with you was just the best. And from then on, my time with you has been the happiest of my life. And I don't want this... us to ever end. I want this forever. I love you so much, I am so in love with you Alison Noelle Stewart. Alison, you're the most incredible girl in the world. You're absolutely beautiful, inside and out. Before I met you, I was afraid to want or hope for anything because I didn't want to get my hopes up to just be disappointed in the end. I thought everything and anything I wanted would never happen for me. But then you came along."

He smiled so big. I can see so much emotion in his eyes. "You made me believe in myself. You let me know that it was okay to hope and dream and want things for myself. You made me realize that I can have anything I want. You made me believe in things that I thought were impossible for myself. You have done so much for me and given so much to me, I only hope I can do half of what you have done for me. Alison Stewart, I love you with all of my heart. You are the most important person to me. Nothing would make me happier than for us to be married, for me to be your husband and for us to finally have that family and life I've been waiting for all my life. And if you say eyes in a minute, I promise to continue adoring you, appreciating everything you do for me, and cherishing the way you make me feel for the rest of our lives."

And then he got down on one knee and revealed a stunning white gold three stone diamond engagement ring. I was mesmerized. It was beautiful and perfect and exactly what I could ever want in an engagement ring. He looked nervous. He looked at me with so much love and bit down on his bottom lip before he asked, "So, will you marry me?"

I certainly didn't see this coming. I had no clue he was going to propose, not until he actually asked me. A whole bunch of different emotions took over my body. I couldn't even bring myself to speak. I just stood there smiling with my mouth wide open in shock. Poor Ryan, he was just anxiously waiting for my answer and I couldn't even get the tiniest voice out of my mouth. I just nodded slowly with the biggest smile plastered all over my face.

"Is that a yes?" he asked, his eyes never leaving mine.

"Yes. Yes. Yes. Yes." I finally said.

He quickly stood up, picked me up in his arms and kissed and kissed me, only stopping to give each other the goofiest grins. This feeling was nothing like I've ever felt before. I can't ever remember being this happy. I just couldn't believe that Ryan and I were engaged. I get to marry my best friend. Life couldn't get any better.

29

EPILOGUE

7 years later
Ryan's POV

I stir the slightest bit only to feel my beautiful wife snuggle closer into my body. Mornings are probably one of my favorite parts of the day. Especially the moment I wake up next to this gorgeous woman right next to me. I pulled her in closer, as if that were even possible. She held onto me tighter as the skin on her smooth warm leg slipped over mine. The moment I open my eyes I see her face. Her eyes were still closed but the smile on her yummy lips and the way her hands and her body moved against mine let me know she was wide awake.

Ahhh, what a way to wake up.

I let my hands wander from the length of her back, over her bottom, and over her thighs. Slowly, I roll over her. Holding myself up with my elbows to keep from squishing her beneath me. But none of that kept her from wrapping her legs around me to pull me closer to her. She opened her eyes, her stunning grey eyes, to give me a cheeky smile. I loved how our mornings started. I bent my head slightly to kiss her. My lips brushed hers ever so slightly before fully capturing her lips with my own. Her hands ran up my back possesively as, what seemed like, every bit of her pulled me closer and closer causing me to groan. I wanted more.

Before we can get on, we hear our bedroom door open. And soon enough, our two perfect children Aiden and Zooey are bouncing on our bed.

Alison giggles under me. She smiles apologetically even though we both love our children. "Time to get up."

I reluctantly roll over and sit up. Although we're disappointed about being interrupted we didn't really mind once we saw those cute little faces.

"Dad, it's Max's birthday party today and I can play Happy Birthday on my guitar." Aiden says with subtle excitement.

"And I can sing it!" Zooey adds loudly as she pulls her mom's arm thinking it would pass on her excitement.

"That's wonderful, guys!" Alison says enthusiastically.

"Let's hear it." I tell them.

Aiden quickly leaves the room to retrieve his guitar and comes back before any of us can do anything. Aiden prepares himself and counts before he strums the first chord. Zooey begins to sing. Both of them focusing on getting it right. I couldn't help but smile. Once they finished, Alison and I clapped proudly. Zooey being the dramatic lively little girl she is takes a bow while Aiden smiles shyly at us.

"Wow, great job guys!" I say truly amazed at how talented our kids are. "Give me a hug, that was amazing." I say as they make there way towards me. They tackle me onto my bed giggling. I look over at Alison smiling thoughtfully at us. This is the family I always wanted. The way our kids looked at me with happy faces because they know they have parents who love them unconditionally made me the happiest man on earth. This is everything I could ever ask for.

We spent the morning preparing for the day. I help Zooey get ready.

"Make sure you finish your oatmeal" I hear my wife say to my son Aiden.

"Okay, mom" Aiden says.

I finish helping Zooey get dressed. She's wearing the white flower dress Alison got her for the millionth time. She twirls and stops only to ask me to brush her hair. She hands me her brush. I quickly comb through her chocolate brown hair, as we're running late, and pull it up into a ponytail. She turns around and beams up at me with the same pair of gorgeous grey eyes her mother has. My little Zooey looks exactly like Alison...beautiful. But her smile fades when she figures out I've given her a ponytail. She was expecting a braid. And of course, only her mother could give her that. But we had no time. We were expected at Kenny and Anna's house to help set up for their son Max's 5th birthday.

Since we graduated college, Anna gave birth to a baby girl named Amanda and two years after that she had Max. As for Alison and I, we've been happily married for six years. We have two children, Aiden and Zooey. I forgot to mention Aiden and Zooey are faternal twins. Alison and I were surprised, to say the least, when we found out wouldn't be having just one child but two. If you think taking care of one baby is tough try raising two. It was double the tantrums, double the dirty diapers, and double everything. Even though it was difficult, we had a lot of help. Anna and Kenny did as much as they could to help us develop a routine. And Alison's parents stayed with us for the first couple of months. But now, Aiden and Zooey are 4 going on 5 years old. They have grown up into a pair wonderful kids.

Both our families moved to LA for work. And now, Alison, Aiden, Zooey and I will be moving to New York next month. I've been offered a job at a communications company and Alison has been extremely supportive the minute I told her about the job. I wasn't going to take it if she didn't want me to but she encouraged me to take it. So I did.

"Daddy, can I have a braid please?" Zooey asks

"Zo, we don't have time." She frowns, "Tell you what, if we can get out that front door in 15 minutes, maybe mommy can –"

"Maybe mommy can what?" Alison asks curiously as she walks into Zooey's almost empty room to put away some clothes.

Before I can tell her, Zooey jumps onto Alison like a monkey and says, "Mommy can you braid my hair if we have 'nuf time?"

"We're running late. We still have to get all the cupcakes packed." I tell her.

"Already done. " My beautiful wife beams at me

"Well then, Zo, looks like you can get your braid." I say and she smiles and claps her hands together in delight.

"Mommy, member when Audrey and I had matching braids?" Zooey asks Alison.

"Sure do. You two looked like twins."

"Uh huh. And she even had a flowery dress too, just like me. 'Cept hers was pink. Member?"

"Yup. Are you excited to see her when we move to New York?" Alison asks

"YES!" Zooey exclaims. "Will she be at Max's party, daddy?"

"No, she won't but you'll see her when we move to New York, you can wait till then right?"

"Uh huh. When we get to New York can Audrey come over and play?" she asks excitedly.

"If it's alright with her parents."

"Really?!" she says with big happy eyes.

Alison and I both laugh and nod. Zooey has grown into such a bubbly, intellectual and sociable young girl. She's always so animated when she speaks just like her mother. When we told her about the move to New York she asked us a billion questions. She was so curious and after she met my boss' daughter Audrey, the prospect of moving only excited her.

"Honey, can you make sure Aiden is all washed up and ready to go?" Alison asks me.

"Yup."

I find my son finishing his oatmeal at the breakfast table. His legs swinging forward and backward under the table. He seemed to be enjoying his breakfast. As I go to the sink to wash the remaining dishes, I ask him, "How's that oatmeal?"

"Good." He replies as he continues to swing his legs.

"You know, I never really liked oatmeal when I was younger." I tell him as I take a seat opposite him.

"It's okay. Mommy says it's good for me." He replies simply. I smiled. He was such a good boy. When we first brought him home from the hospital all he would do was sleep and wake up only when he was hungry. Over the years he came into his own. He didn't speak much but he wasn't guarded or secretive either. He was just quiet. He liked to observe and try things on his own. He was very different from Zooey.

"She's right." I say. "You know, you're such a good kid."

"Thanks" he smiles

"You're the best son I've ever had"

He wrinkles his nose and says, "I'm your only son, dad." I laugh too as he finished the last of his oatmeal.

"All done?" I ask. He nods and hands me the bowl and spoon. " Go get your jacket on we're leaving soon."

"Okay." He leaves and comes back shortly to ask me to help him put on his jacket.

15 minutes later and we're in the car on the way to Anna and Kenny's. Once we arrive we help set up the decorations. Amanda, Max, Aiden and Zooey are enjoying the bouncy jumper while we set up.

"How's the packing going?" Anna asks

Alison's POV

"We're about done. We just need to get the kids' rooms packed. It's a little crazy seeing the house filled with nothing but boxes. It looks exactly like it did when we first moved in, aside from that God awful green carpet." I say.

Anna covers her face with her hand remembering the carpet, "Oh my god. That carpet! It was just horrible."

"Tell me about it. Thank god, Aiden tipped over the paint can and stained that carpet. Or else we'd be stuck with it."

"Hey, we were saving for a new couch remember?" Ryan defends himself because he refused to pay to get the carpet removed and put in wood floors. I know it would be a bit costly to get wood floors but that carpet was just ugly, old, and dirty. But he was right. We needed a new couch first. But none of that matters anymore. That paint stain stuck to the carpet and it remained there until Ryan couldn't stand looking at it much longer. Three days after the paint stain the carpet Ryan called for an estimate for wood floors. I smile to myself remembering.

"Yeah, I remember." I say

"But we did have some great memories with that carpet. Like Aiden and his first steps." He reminds me.

"Oh yeah. Remember him wobbling and swaying from side to side?"

Kenny laughs, "He looked drunk."

We all laugh and then it became silent. Each one of us was reminiscing about the past five years. Lots of memories were made in that house. We were all fortunate to have learned about parenthood together. This is where our families started and now we were leaving to a new place to start all over again. To make new memories.

Once we snapped out of it we continued to get ready for the party. I looked at Ryan. Not much has changed about him in the past 7 years. He was just as sweet, thoughtful and caring as the first time we met. We've been married for six years and everyday I learn new things about him. I fall in love with him every single day. He is an amazing husband and an incredible dad. And I can't wait to spend the next however many years we have with this man and our children.

Aiden and Zooey had so much fun at Max's party that they have exhausted themselves to sleep on the car ride home. We carry Zooey and Aiden into their rooms we tuck them in and kiss them good night. As I slowly and quietly close Zooey's door as to not wake her, Ryan slips his arms around me from behind. He nuzzles his face into my neck making me sigh. He reluctantly let go enough for us to head downstairs to the living room.

We settled onto the couch and cuddled up. I settled into the right side of his body. He pulled me in with his strong arms and immediately I felt warm inside. He always gave me a sense of safety and comfort when he held me and this time was no different. He inhaled deeply and I felt his chest well up against my face. I could hear his heart beating steadily.

"Ry, this is our last month in this house." I whisper.

Looking around, seeing our boxes stacked up around the room made our house, our home feel less like our home. We had so many firsts here with our family. Aiden and Zooey took there first steps here. We marked their heights in the coat closet by the door. This house that I thought we'd live in until our children were grown is slowly slipping away. In a month this home won't be ours anymore. And although, I agreed to move to New York it doesn't make me miss this place any less.

He tilted his head to study my face, "Are you having second thoughts about moving?" he asked worried.

I rubbed his forearm to reassure him I wasn't, "No, honey. I'm not. I just... It's going to be difficult saying goodbye to this place. This home is where we started our family. It's going to be hard to let go."

He pulled me in closer to place a kiss on my forehead, "I know. I'm going to miss this place too. We have a lot of memories here. We may have to move to a different house but we'll make that house our home like we did here. Wherever we live, we'll make our own memories and we can remember them forever. We don't ever have to forget our memories."

I turn to look at him and give him a kiss, he smiled against my lips, "You always know what to say to make me feel better."

"I can say the same about you." He tucked a strand of hair behind my ear, "You've done it for me many times before. We pick each other up because we're a team, you and I."

"You're great."

"Just great?" he asked with a grin.

"No, better than great. You're my incredible best friend and I love you."

Then he gave me a sweet and slow kiss. "I love you too."